The Book of Causes

[*Liber de Causis*]

Translated from the Latin
With an Introduction

by

DENNIS J. BRAND

MARQUETTE UNIVERSITY PRESS
MILWAUKEE, WISCONSIN 53233

© Copyright, 1981, 1984, Dennis J. Brand

First Edition, 1981*
Second Edition, Revised, 1984

Printed in the United States of America

ISBN 0-87462-225-5

Library of Congress Catalogue Card Number: 84-61118

* The first edition of *Liber de Causis* was published by the Niagara University Press
as part of a series dedicated to Jacques and Raissa Maritain.

Robert Engbring
Director Marquette University Press

Table of Contents

Foreword

One of the central documents in the dossier on Neo-Platonism in the Middle Ages is, unquestionably, the *Liber de causis*. Although doubts still linger about the origin and authorship of this opuscule, no one would think of minimizing its doctrinal importance in the history of medieval metaphysics. Slipped (by accident?) into the catalogue the Arabs had of Aristotle's works, the *Liber* became, together with the *Theology of Aristotle*, one of the principal sources of the eclectic tendency of Arabic and Jewish metaphysics. The Latins of the 13th Century, who did not have access to the *Theology of Aristotle*, did have knowledge of the *Liber de causis*, thanks to the translation made by Gerard of Cremona in Toledo. Circulated under Aristotle's name, this opuscule allowed the medievals to fill the metaphysical lacunae the authentic works of the Stagirite presented *vis-à-vis* the vision of the world inspired by the great monotheistic religions. From the end of the 12th Century, the Latin theologians began to make use of the *Liber*. Alan of Lille, in his *Contra hereticos*, seems to have been the first to use it. In the first quarter of the 13th Century, Alexander of Hales and Roland of Cremona worked on this treatise. As early as 1230-40, the *De causis* figured, along with the *Metaphysica vetus* and the *Metaphysica nova*, among the texts of First Philosophy that a student of Arts at the University of Paris was supposed to read.

Despite the interdictions that hung over the *libri naturales* of Aristotle (among which was numbered the *Liber de causis*), this opuscule continued to enjoy a growing success. Roger Bacon — always so independent — took it as the subject for his lectures around 1245. Even before him at Oxford, where the proscriptions of Paris did not apply, the *Liber de causis* was taught by Alexander Neckham, Adam of Buckfield, and Thomas of York. Its official ratification as a fundamental source for philosophical studies, however, took place on March 19, 1255, when it became, according to new statutes, a text for required reading at the Faculty of Arts at Paris. From this date, every professor was required to devote seven weeks to the reading and exposition of the *De causis*. Albert the Great, Thomas Aquinas, Siger of Brabant, and Giles of Rome wrote important commentaries on the text. But by Albert's time, the question of the authenticity of the opuscule was already being raised. The question was inevitable, for a better understanding of the Aristotelian system, resulting from a longer acquaintance with the texts of the Stagirite, was beginning to bear witness to the differences in the presuppositions that guided authentic Aristotelian thought and the Neo-Platonic philosophy of the *Liber de causis*.

Finally, it was St. Thomas who signaled the true origin of the opuscule: he recognized in it theses extracted from Proclus' *Elements of Theology*. Three quarters of a century of confusion was thus ended. But the fact that it was no longer reckoned among the writings of Aristotle did not diminish the authority or the importance of the *Liber de causis*. It continued to be, along with Avicenna, Ibn Gabirol, Pseudo-Dionysius, and St. Augustine, one of the principal sources of the Neo-Platonism that so profoundly personalized the Aristotelian basis common to medieval philosophers. As such, the *Liber* presents itself as an inevitable object of reflection for all historians who wish to understand the fundamental tendencies of medieval thought and of the Neo-Platonizing Aristotelianism that seems to mark all of the great thinkers of the 13th Century, including St. Thomas. The study of these tendencies and of the Neo-Platonic inspiration of medieval philosophy seems to be one of the most promising lines of research leading to a better understanding of Western thought.

Translations have always played an extremely important role in beginning the process of assimilation of one historical culture by another. Such was the case with the Arabs in the 9th Century, with the Latins in the 12th and 13th Century, as well as in the Renaissance. On each occasion, the translation of fundamental texts sparked a movement of reflection that has enriched philosophical life. Our era has continued this tradition, so it is that philologists have bequeathed us versions of the principal sources of philosophy in almost every modern language. With regard to the *Liber de causis*, however, English-language researchers were at a disadvantage. The French have at their disposal the Arabico-French translation of Fr. G.C. Anawati; the Poles, that of the Akademia Teologii Katolickiej of Warsaw. Likewise, the Japanese have had a translation since 1967, thanks to the efforts of K. Oshika. The time has come to make available an English version of this fundamental text. The work of Dennis J. Brand fills this gap, meeting the research and teaching needs of the English-language medievalist.

Translation, of course, is but the *point of departure* for the work of reflection upon and assimilation of a text. Its principal merit is to initiate discussion of the deepest meaning of a treatise. Let us not forget that all translation is already an interpretation. The properly hermeneutical dimension, therefore, begins with the translation and continues as a fruitful dialogue between philosophers, historians, and philologists. It is for this reason that Mr. Brand has chosen to remain as close to the text as the spirit of the English language will allow. He thus offers us a faithful and intelligent translation of the *Latin* text edited by Fr. A. Pattin. This work, then, is a translation of a translation. And so it holds a twofold interest, for it testifies both to the difficulties encountered by the Latins in translating the Arabic and to the problems encountered today in expressing in a modern idiom all the richness of the central metaphysical intuitions of Neo-Plationism. The contribution of Mr. Brand will be, without a doubt, warmly welcomed by historians of Latin and Arabic thought, for he has been able to surmount the difficulties of his task, while retaining the flavor (and the rigor) of the medieval version.

Bernardo Carlos Bazán
University of Ottawa

Translator's Introduction

A. Title, Date, Authorship

Little by little, contemporary historians[1] are penetrating the mystery surrounding the origins of *The Book of Causes*. The treatise seems to have been widely known and circulated from the beginning of the 13th Century in Latin translation, under two titles: *Liber Aristotelis de expositione bonitatis purae* and *Liber de causis*. As such, it has been preserved in over 230 manuscripts. Since the pioneering studies of O. Bardenhewer[2] and M. Steinschneider,[3] historians unanimously recognize that the Medieval Latin translation was originally made in the Mozarabic city of Toledo by Gerard of Cremona (d. 1187) from an Arabic exemplar. Indeed, a treatise with the title *Liber de expositione bonitatis purae* is included in a list of works translated by Gerard into Latin.[4] More recently, Adriaan Pattin[5] has published a philological study indicating that the text exhibits evidence of the Latin vocabulary characteristic of Dominic Gundisalvi, Gerard of Cremona's co-translator at Toledo. Pattin concludes that the data point not to two chronologically and substantially different texts, but rather to one basic text translated by Gerard and in places revised by Dominic. With regard, however, to the prehistory of the *Liber de causis*, that is, its authorship, date and place of composition, and even the original language of composition, there has been much conjecture and difference of opinion.

This contemporary confusion parallels the state of the question in the Medieval Latin world.[6] At different times during the Middle Ages, paternity of the treatise was variously attributed to Theophrastus (d. 286 B.C.); Avicenna (d. 1037); Algazel (d. 1111); and to Aristotle (d. 322 B.C.); with or without commentary by Alfarabi (d. 950). By the early 1230s, Aristotle's candidature held ascendancy over all others. Thus, when the University of Paris lifted the proscriptions against the *libri naturales* of the Stagrite in 1255, the *Liber de causis* was officially enrolled into the syllabus of the Faculty of Arts as a canonical work of Aristotle under the title *Liber Aristotelis de expositione bonitatis purae.*[7]

Not long thereafter, two Dominican Regent Masters in the Faculty of Theology at Paris challenged the attribution of the *De causis* to Aristotle. Friar Albert of Cologne attributed the *Liber* to David the Jew, who is known to contemporary historians as Ibn Daoud or Avendauth (fl. 1150). And Friar Thomas d'Aquino, after reading Proclus' *Elements of Theology* in the Latin translation made in 1268 by Friar William of Moerbeke, concluded that the *Liber de causis* was translated from an Arabic work based upon Proclus' *Elements.*[8] Aquinas' discovery effectively eliminated the paternity of Aristotle and Theophrastus, but left unaffected Alberts' opinion. Furthermore, Thomas' observation that the *Liber* was translated from an Arabic exemplar did not eliminate the possibility that the text might have been first written in a different language and subsequently translated into Arabic. It could have been written in Syriac, for example, like the so-called *Theology of Aristotle*, which in fact is an epitome of Plotinus' *Enneads*.

In addition to the Latin translation, manuscripts exist in Arabic, Armenian, and Hebrew. Bardenhewer opined that Arabic was the original language of composition. His Arabic text was based on the only complete codex then known.[9] Subsequently, another Arabic codex was discovered by Professor F. Sezgin.[10] The Hebrew translation has been documented by M. Steinschneider.[11] Much of the disagreement between scholars can be attributed to the incomplete state of the manuscript traditions.

Contemporary historians writing on the origins of the treatise separate basically into two schools: Arabists and Latinists. The Arabists attribute the text to an anonymous author who lived during the 9th or 10th Century and who worked in the cultural milieu that radiated from Baghdad. Possibly the author worked at the center for translation of Greek works into Arabic and Syriac founded in 832 by Caliph al-Ma'mum.[12] Included among the Arabists are: Bardenhewer,[13] Kraus,[14] d'Alverny,[15] Walzer,[16] Anawati,[17] Saffrey,[18] and Badawi.[19] Since no Arab author before the 12th Century mentions the *Liber*, the Latinists are convinced that the treatise did not spring from Eastern soil. Rather, they assign the origins of the *De causis* to one of the two frontiers between the Latin and Arab worlds: most probably Spain and in particular Toledo, where it was translated, or possibly the Kingdom of Sicily. Among the Latinists (and those who are expert in the Hebrew tradition) are: Steinschneider,[20] Kaufmann,[21] Guttmann,[22] Duhem,[23] Alónso,[24] and Pattin.[25]

A brief and partial glance at the divergent opinions and dialogue between two prominent scholars may serve to highlight the differences between Latinists and Arabists. Fr. A. Pattin,[26] in accordance with the attribution made by the Bodleian Library manuscript[27] and the testimony of Albertus Magnus[28] as well as others, attributes authorship to Ibn Daoud, a contemporary of Gerard and Dominic in Toledo. Fr. H.D. Saffrey[29] has leveled several criticisms against Pattin's thesis. He objects, for example, that Ibn Daoud, who was a rather modest figure, did not know enough Greek to work on the text of Proclus. Furthermore, Saffrey wonders why, if Ibn Daoud were the author of the text and since he was present in Toledo when Gerard made the Latin translation, there are the two Arabic words, *achili* and *yliathim*, left untranslated in the Latin text. And, because he discerns an affinity between the vocabulary and doctrine of *The Book of Causes* and the soi-disant *Theology of Aristotle* he contends that there is an affinity in their origins as well.

Pattin[30] responds to Saffrey's objections: Supposing gratuitously that Ibn Daoud did not know enough Greek to read Proclus' *Elements*, it is not inconceivable that he had access to an Arabic translation or excerpts of that work. As to the Arabic transcription of two words in the Latin text, this is easily explained by the fact that Ibn Daoud would have drafted his work for his Arabic coreligionaries; and, when Gerard had seen how successful the treatise was, he took it upon himself to translate it, without the assistance of the author.

While there has not been universal agreement about the identity of the author of *The Book of Causes*, further information about him has been gleaned from the doctrinal studies of his treatise. G.C. Anawati[31] and others have contended that, besides access to Proclus as the main source of the *Liber*, the author had access to Plotinus' *Enneads*. Fr. Leo Sweeney[32] in his study of creation in the *De causis* has demonstrated that the author was a monotheistic creationist, who transformed the Procline doctrine of emanation into a true doctrine of divine creation and providence. In the same study, he noted the similarity between the two moments in the emanation of plurality from the One as taught by Plotinus in the *Enneads* and in the creation of all things by the One-True-God as taught in the *Liber*, thus providing additional evidence for the contention that the author had access to the *Enneads* in one form or another.

B. Significance of the Text

The significance of the *Liber de causis* for contemporary historians is twofold, for the treatise exercised a double influence on medieval thought: literary and doctrinal. The opuscule is divided into 31(32) propositions, or chapters, containing a total of 219 apophthegms. Its structure is similar to that of its principal source, the *Elements of Theology,* in that both endeavor to establish demonstrations *more geometrico* of the propositions enunciated. As with the argumentation of the *Elements,* however, many of the would-be demonstrations of the *Liber* are more properly systematic commentaries than strict *a priori* deductions. The importance of this literary form for the medievals has been signaled by Professor Etienne Gilson:

> From the point of view of literary form, they [the propositions] have favored the development of the aphoristic style of which Boethius and Alan of Lille had already given striking examples. Every time a philosphical or theological opuscule consists of concise aphoristic statements, often alliterative, and attended or not by a short commentary, the influence of the *Book of Causes* can at least be suspected.[33]

The aphoristic style also favored a wider dissemination of the though of the *Liber.* Many of the axioms[34] of the opuscule became current coin during the succeeding years. Propositions such as "The first of things created is being" (Prop. 37) and "The First Cause is above all description" (Prop. 57) were unhesitatingly accepted and frequently repeated, even by those who did not embrace the entire doctrine of the *De causis.*

It was, however, in its doctrinal content that *The Book of Causes* made its principal impact on the Scholastics of the Latin West. Few Schoolmen did not incorporate at least some of the metaphysics of the *Liber* into their personal syntheses. While the medievals were the philosophical heirs of Aristotle, they were nonetheless in possession of a patrimony of persistent and pervasive Neo-Platonism bequeathed by Augustine, Pseudo-Dionysius, Avicenna, and to a lesser extent by Ibn Gabirol. The *De causis* is a central part of this Neo-Platonic heritage. Despite the striking similarities between the *Liber* and the *Elements,* the two works differ in several fundamental respects.[35] While the *Elements of Theology* is in a very real sense a systematic *summa* of pagan Neo-Platonism, *The Book of Causes,* on the contrary, is an epitome of monotheistic Neo-Platonism. The reinterpretation of Proclus' thought along lines consonant with divine revelation is perhaps the single most important factor for the profound influence exerted by the *De causis* on the metaphysical speculation of the period.

The author of the *Liber* does not present any *divisio textus* of his own, nor does the treatise have any strict organization or structure that unifies the propositions. Nevertheless, in a good example of a *reverenter expositio* of a text, St. Thomas Aquinas suggests the following outline for the treatise, based upon the Neo-Platonic conception of causality and the higher realities of the Neo-Platonic universe.[36]

St. Thomas' Outline of the *Liber De Causis*

The purpose of this work is to give an explanation of the first causes of things.

I. GENERAL PRINCIPLE: The Gradation of Causes: [Prop. 1/I]
  A. The first cause flows over more into the effect than the second cause
  B. The impression of the first cause recedes more slowly from the effect
  C. The impression of the first cause comes to the effect prior to the impression of the second cause

II. THE FIRST CAUSES OF THINGS [Props. 2-32/II-XXXI]
  A. Distinctions Concerning First Causes [Props. 2-15/II-XIV]
    1. Division of first causes [Props. 2-5/II-IV]
    2. Explanation of individual causes [Props. 6-15/V-XIV]
  B. Coordination or Interdependence of Causes
  [Props. 16-32/XV-XXXI]
    1. How lower causes depend from higher causes
    [Props. 16-19/XV-XVIII]
    2. How higher causes flow over into lower causes
    [Props. 20-23/XIX-XXII]
    3. How lower causes diversely receive the effluence from the First Cause [Props. 24-32/XXIII-XXXI]

* * *

A. DISTINCTIONS CONCERNING FIRST CAUSES [Props. 2-15/II-XIV]
  1. Division of First Causes: [Props. 2-5/II-IV]
    a) Division into three grades: [Prop. 2/II]
      (1) First Cause = God
      (2) Intelligences
      (3) Souls

How first causes are united through participation in the highest cause
[Prop. 3/III]
      b) Division of Intelligences [Prop. 4/IV]
      c) Division of Souls [Prop. 5/IV]

  2. Explanation of Individual Causes: [Props. 6-15/V-XIV]
      a) First Cause [Prop. 6/V]
      b) Intelligence: [Props. 7-13/VI-XII]
        (1) Substance of Intelligence [Prop. 7/VI]
        (2) Knowledge of Intelligence: [Props. 8-13/VII-XII]
          (a) How Intelligence knows the other:
             [Props. 8-12/VII-XI]
             (i)   higher and lower causes [Prop. 8/VII]
             (ii) the cause above itself [Prop. 9/VIII]
             (iii) in general: how Intelligence understands the
                   other [Prop. 10/IX]
             (iv) in particular:
                 (α) how Intelligence knows eternal things
                     [Prop. 11/X]
                 (β) how eternal things mutually understand
                     one another [Prop. 12/XI]
          (b) Self-understanding of Intelligence [Prop. 13/XII]
      c) Soul: [Props. 14-15/XIII-XIV]
        (1) In relation to others [Prop. 14/XIII]
        (2) In itself [Prop. 15/XIV]

B. COORDINATION OR INTERDEPENDENCE OF CAUSES
  [Props. 16-32/XV-XXXI]
  1. How Lower Causes Depend from Higher Causes
    [Props. 16-19/XV-XVIII]
      a) With respect to power: [Props. 16-17/XV-XVI]
        (1) Every infinite power depends from the First Infiinite
           Power [Prop. 16/XV]
        (2) How powers are more or less assimilated to the First
           Infinite Power [Prop. 17/XVI]

      b) With respect to substance and nature:
        [Props. 18-19/XVII-XVIII]
        (1) How things depend universally from the First Cause
           [Prop. 18/XVII]

As the above division of the text clearly shows, for the author of *The Book of Causes,* the universe is a cosmos, that is, a world-system structured according to the basic metaphysical laws of Neo-Platonism. The first and most fundamental of these is the principle of causality. The universe is, in fact, an ensemble of causes and effects — of primary and secondary causes, of higher and lower causes. Primary causes have a greater influence and comprehension than secondary causes. They are the cause of all other causes and of their effects as well. Thus, primary causes are the first to extend their power to effects and the last to withdraw it from them. There are three primary causes, which are *per se* causes. These correspond to the traditional hypotheses that constitute the Neo-Platonic hierarchy, namely, the First Cause, Intelligence, and Soul. The First Cause is unequivocally the blessed and sublime God of a monotheist believer. God is before eternity, above being, absolutely transcendent, beyond all knowledge and description. The First Cause, nevertheless, extends his causal influence to all things, for he creates all things (gives being to them), overflows perfections upon them, and rules them with an absolute providence. The First Cause is Goodness and Richness itself, and he outpours all perfections uniformly with but one effluence. The diversity of perfections and gifts comes not from the One-True-God, but rather from the recipients, who are manifold. The First Cause creates being first and directly. The First Created Being is Intelligence. Intelligence is coexistent with eternity, on a par with it. Together with Soul, Intelligence is self-constituted, that is, through contemplation of the First Cause, Intelligence and Soul fill themselves with perfection. In the language of the Schoolmen, the Intelligences are the separate substances or angels. They are simple, incorporeal substances, who understand themselves without discursive reasoning, without movement or extension. Intelligence is subdivided and arranged hierarchically, with the First Divine Intelligence in the lead position and mere or bare Intelligences at the lowest level. It is through the intermediation of the Intelligences that the creative force of the First Cause extends to other things.

As the hierarchy of prime causes declines towards Nature, Soul comes between Intelligence and Nature. Soul is on the horizon of being, because it is attached to eternity from below and yet is above time. Soul is the bridge between time and eternity, between Intelligence and Nature. The First Cause posited Soul as the stratum on which Intelligence performs its activity. Once again, Souls are subdivided and hierarchically ordered, with the lead position being occupied by the First Intellectual Soul and the lowest position by mere Souls. Below Soul is Nature, the sensible universe. The highest position in Nature goes to Heavenly Bodies and Time, and the lowest to sensible matter.

Even from this cursory glance, it is obvious that there are complex interrelations other than that of causality obtaining between the different levels and within each of the levels of reality, e.g., inexistence or a kind of ontological imbrication, triadic divisions and mutual resemblances, etc. These relationships are, as Fr. Sweeney has observed,[37] all the more difficult to understand due to the brevity of the treatise, the profundity of the thought, and the several apparent contradictions in the text.

C. Text and Translation

1. Latin Edition:

I have made this translation from the Latin edition established by Adriaan Pattin, O.M.I.:

> "Le *Liber de causis*. Édition établie à l'aide de 90 manuscrits avec introduction et notes." *Tijdschrift voor Filosofie* 28 (1966): 90-203. Also published separately: Louvain: Éditions du "Tijdschrift voor Filosofie," n.d. [1966]. My citations are of the former.

In preparing his edition, Fr. Pattin thoroughly collated 10 manuscripts and consulted 82 others, comparing them to the editions of Bardenhewer, Steele, the paraphrases of Albert the Great, the lemmata found in the commentary of Thomas Aquinas, as well as the edition of the *Liber* included in the commentary of Giles of Rome in the printed edition of the 1550 (see below). Notwithstanding all his efforts, Fr. Pattin acknowledges that his text is not to be considered the definitive critical edition of the *De causis*. He states that his purpose is more limited, to present "an intelligible and sufficiently correct text." In this he has succeeded. Nonetheless, the scholarly value of Fr. Pattin's edition can be seen from the two apparatus he provides: textual variants and explanatory notes. Canon Fernand Van Steenberghen has aptly characterized Fr. Pattin's work. "Without being critical in the strict sense, his edition is excellent and largely sufficient."[38] Fr. Pattin's Latin edition is, at least for the present, the best one available.

My relation to Fr. Pattin's Latin text is much the same as his relation to the manuscript tradition. I realize that I have not been working with the critical edition, and so my purpose is rather modest. I have tried to make available to those with an interest in medieval studies but who do not handle any Latin a reasonable English translation of this seminal philosophical work from an "excellent and largely sufficient text." I have endeavored to give an intelligent and intelligible translation of that text without departing too much from the style of the Latin, albeit often an awkward and repetitious style — awkward because it frequently reflects the grammar of the Arabic original, and repetitious because it is written *more geometrico*. I have not considered, therefore, even in the most problematical instances translating with a variant to Fr. Pattin's established text, preferring to rely on his critical judgment and leaving aside questions of textual criticisms, emendations, etc.

In his recently completed doctoral dissertation on the Arabic *De causis,* Richard C. Taylor has devoted an appendix to 231 critical observations and remarks on the Latin *Liber:*

> TAYLOR, Richard C. "The *Liber de causis (Kalam fi mahd al-khair):* A Study of Medieval Neoplatonism." Ph.D. dissertation, University of Toronto, 1981.

Dr. Taylor has announced that he is currently preparing two separate editions of *The Book of Causes:* the critical Latin edition of the *Liber de causis* and the critical Arabic edition of the *Kalam fi mahd al-khair* [Discourse on the pure good].

2. Arabic Editions:

As Dr. Taylor's Latin text will up-date Fr. Pattin's edition, his Arabic text will replace the two previous Arabic texts of Bardenhewer and Badawi, both of which are based upon a unique manuscript (Goluis 209 of the Bibliotheek der Rijksuniversiteit in Leiden):

> BARDENHEWER, Otto. *Die pseudo-aristotelische Schrift Ueber das reine Gute bekannt unter dem Namen Liber de causis.* Freiburg im Breisgau: Herder'sche Verlagshandlung, 1882.

Bardenhewer's work also contains a German "paraphrase" (translation) of the Arabic text as well as an edition of Gerard of Cremona's Latin translation.

> BADAWI, 'Abdurrahmān. *Neoplatonici apud Arabes.* Islamica, 19. *"Procli: Liber (Pseudo-Aristotelis) de expositione bonitatis purae (Liber de causis)."* Cairo, 1955, pp. 1-33.

In making my translation, especially in the preparation of the notes to the text, I have consulted a number of translations, commentaries, and related works as follows:

3. Translations:

In addition to Bardenhewer's Arabico-German translation, I have used the Arabico-French translation of Fr. Anawati:

> ANAWATI, Marie-Marcel (G.C.), O.P. *Liber de causis. Traduction française inédite faite sur le texte arabe édité par Otto Bardenhewer* . . . . Pro manuscripto. Montreal: Institut d'etudes medievales, Université de Montréal, 1950.

Since I do not read Arabic, I have had to make my comparisons of the Latin text with the Arabic edition of Bardenhewer through the intermediary of Bardenhewer's German paraphrases and, especially, Anawati's French translation. This "comparison by dichotomy" means that I am completely indebted to Bardenhewer and Anawati for my understanding of the Arabic text.

Although I was unable to profit from them, I should like to call attention to the Polish and Japanese translations of the Latin *De causis:*

> *Ksiega o Przyczynach* [The book of causes]. Warsaw: Akademia Theologii Katolickiej, 1970.
>
> POULIOT, V.M. and OSHIKA, K. *Liber de causis et Sancti Thomae de Aquino super Librum de causis expositio denuo edidit V.M. Pouliot . . . diligenti cum cooperatione Kazumasa Oshika. In Textus philosophici in linguam japonicam translati cura Instituti Sancti Thomae de Aquino de Kyoto.* Kyoto, 1967.

It is of interest to note that an Italian translation is currently in preparation.

4. Commentaries:

> [ALBERT THE GREAT]. *B. Alberti Magni . . . opera omnia, cura ac labore Augusti Borgnet.* 38 vols. Paris: Vives, 1890-99. Vol. 10 *"Liber de causis et processu universitatis,"* pp. 361-619.
>
> [THOMAS AQUINAS]. *Sancti Thomae de Aquino super Librum de causis expositio.* Critical edition by Henri-Dominique Saffrey, O.P. Fribourg: Société philosophique; Louvain: Éditions E. Nauwelaerts, 1954.
>
> [ROGER BACON] *Quaestiones supra Librum de causis.* In *Opera hactenus inedita Rogeri Baconi,* Fasc. 12. Edited by Robert Steele. Oxford: Clarendon Press, 1935.
>
> [GILES OF ROME]. *Fundatissimi Aegidii Romani, archiepiscopi Bituricensis, doctorum praecipui, ordinis Eremitarum Sancti Augustini, opus super authorem de causis, Alpharabium. Reverendi fratris Aegidii Bonsi Florentini Eremitae Augustiniani opera nunc imprimendum traditum . . .* Venice: J. Zoppin, 1550.
>
> [HENRY OF GHENT]. *Les Quaestiones in Librum de causis attribuées à Henri de Gand.* Critical edition by John P. Zwaenepoel,

C.I.C.M. Louvain: Publications universitaires de Louvain; Paris: Béatrice-Nauwelaerts, 1974.

[SIGER OF BRABANT]. *Les Quaestiones super Librum de causis de Siger de Brabant.* Critical edition by Antonio Marlasca. Louvain: Publications universitaires de Louvain; Paris: Béatrice-Nauwelaerts, 1972.

5. Related Works:

PROCLUS. *The Elements of Theology.* A Revised Text, with Translation, Introduction, and Commentary by E.R. Dodds. 2nd ed. Oxford: Oxford University Press, 1963.

VANSTEENKISTE, C. "Procli *Elementatio theologica* translata a Guilelmo de Moerbeke." *Tijdschrift voor Filosofie* 13 (1951): 263-302; 491-531.

D. Conventions:

{ } are used, following Pattin, to indicate additions to the Latin text that are not contained in Bardenhewer's Arabic text.

(...) are used, following Pattin, to indicate lacunae in the Latin text with respect to Bardenhewer's Arabic text.

[ ] are used to indicate additions to the text that I have occasionally supplied for the sake of clarification.

p stands for Pattin's Latin text.

a stands for Anawati's French translation of the Arabic.

b stands for Bardenhewer's German paraphrases of the Arabic.

d stands for Dodd's edition of Proclus' *Elements of Theology.*

Pattin's division of the text into 31 propositions, following Bardenhewer's Arabic text, is indicated by the use of Roman numerals within the text. The Roman numerals enclosed within the parentheses ( ) indicate the alternate division of the text into 32 propositions, resulting from the division of Proposition IV into two parts, as found in many of the Latin manuscripts.

5. Acknowledgments

I would like to express my gratitude to Dr. Robert W. Engbring, Director, Marquette University Press and to Professor James H. Robb, Editor, Mediaeval Philosophical Texts in Translation series for their encouragement and help in the publication of the present edition.

Special thanks is due to Professor Bernardo Carlos Bazán of the Department of Philosophy, University of Ottawa, for his valuable assistance in improving the accuracy of this translation., Likewise, I am grateful to Rev. Donald. W. Hendricks, Pastor, St. Anthony of Padua Church, Yonkers, New York, for his critical suggestions.

Needless to say, any errors or deficiencies that remain are my own.

Dennis J. Brand
Milwaukee, Wisconsin
U.S.A.
May 1984

Notes

1. For a comprehensive view of the *status quaestionis* see the following surveys: H. Bédoret, "L'auteur et le traducteur du *Liber de causis*," *Revue néoscolastique de philosophie* 41 (1938): 519-33; C.G. Anawati, "Prolégomènes à une nouvelle édition du *De causis* arabe," in *Mélanges Louis Massignon*, vol 1(Damascus, 1956), pp. 73-110; H.D. Saffrey, "L'état actuel des recherches sur le *Liber de causis* comme source de la métaphysique au moyen âge," in *Miscellanea Mediaevalia*, vol. 2 (Berlin, 1963), pp. 267-81; G.C. Anawati, "Le néoplatonisme dans la pensée musulmane: état actuel des rechereches, " in *Etudes de philosophie musulmane* (Paris, 1974), pp. 168-77.

2. O. Bardenhewer, *Die pseudo-aristotelische Schrift Ueber das reine Gute bekannt unter dem Namen Liber de causis* (Freiburg im Breisgau, 1882).

3. M. Steinschneider, *Catalogus librorum hebraeorum in bibliotheca Bodleiana* (Berlin, 1852-60), pp. 742ff.

4. Vatican, *Bibl. Apost. Vat. lat.* 2392, ff 97vb-98ra. This list has also been published in B. Boncompagni, *Della vita e della opere di Gherardo Cremonese, traduttore del secolo duodecimo, e di Gherardo da Sabbionetta, astronomo del secolo decimoterzo* (Rome, 1851).

5. A. Pattin, "Over de schrijver en de vertaler van het *Liber de causis*," *Tijdschrift voor Filosofie* 23 (1961): 503-26. See also the argument summarized in A. Pattin, "Le *Liber de causis*," *Tijdschrift voor Filosofie* 28 (1966): 90-102.

6. A. Pattin, *Tijdschrift voor Filosofie* 28 (1966): 90-2 has called attention to the summary of the state of the question during the Middle Ages given by the anonymous author of the commentary on the *Liber* found in Vienna, *Nationalbibliothek lat.* 5500, ff 47r-63r. See also : R. Murari "Il *De causis* e la sua fortuna nel medio evo," *Giornale storico della litteratura italiana* 34 (1899): 98-117.

7. Chartularium Universitatis Parisiensis, edited by H. Denifle and A. Chatelain, vol. 1 (Paris 1889), p. 278.

8. Sancti Thomae de Aquino Super Librum de causis exposito, edited by H.D. Saffrey (Louvain, 1954), *Prooemium*, p. 3, lines 5-8.

9. Leiden, *Bibliotheek der Rijksuniversiteit,* Golius 209, dated 1197. P. Kraus also found the same text in Cairo codex *Taymūr Hikma* 117, dated 1529; see P. Kraus, "Plotin chez les Arabes," *Bulletin de l'Institut d'Egypte* 23 (1941): 263-95, especially 279 ff.

10. Ankara, *Bibliothèque de Saib* 1696, ff 78r-90v, dated from the 15th Century.

11. M. Steinschneider, *Op. Cit.*

12. For a discussion of the center of translation in Baghdad see F.E. Peters, *Aristotle and the Arabs* (New York, 1968), ch. 3: "The Eastern Translation Movement," pp. 57-67.

13. O. Bardenhewer, *Op. Cit.*

14. P. Kraus, *Op. Cit.*

15. M.T. d'Alverny, "Avendauth?" in *Homenaje a Millas-Villacrosa*, vol. 1 (Barcelona, 1954), pp. 19-43.

16. R. Walzer, in *Encyclopédie de l'Islam*, vol. 1 (Leyden; Paris, 1960), 1380-81.

17. G.C. Anawati, "Prolégomènes. . .," *Op. Cit.* and "Le néoplatonisme. . .," *Op. Cit.*

18. H.D. Saffrey, *"L'état actuel. . .," Op. Cit.*

19. A. Badawi, *La transmission de la philosophie grecque au monde arabe* (Paris, 1968).

20. M. Steinschneider, *Op. Cit.*

21. D. Kaufmann, Review of O. Bardenhewer, *Op. Cit.* in *Gottingische gelehrte Anzeigen* 1 (1883): 536-67.

22. J. Guttmann, *Die Scolastik der drizenten Jahrhunderts in ihren Beziehungen zum Judenthum und zur judischen Litteratur* (Breslau, 1902), pp. 54-5.

23. P. Duhem, *Le système du monde,* vol. 4 (Paris 1916), pp. 329-347.

24. M. Alonso, "El *Liber de causis,*" *Al-Andalus* 9 (1944): 43-69; and "Las fuentes literarias del *Liber de causis,*" *Al-Andalus* 10 (1945): 345-82.

25. A. Pattin, "Over de schrijver. . .," *Op. Cit.;* and "Le *Liber de causis,*" *Op. Cit.*

26. A. Pattin, "Over de schrijver. . .," *Op. Cit.*

27. Oxford, *Bodleian Library, Selden sup.* 24, ff 76r-83v.

28. Vatican, *Bibl. Apost. Vat. lat.* 717, f 14r.

29. H.D. Saffrey, L'état. . .," *Op. Cit.,*

30. A. Pattin, "Le *Liber de causis,*" *Op. Cit.,* pp. 92-8.

31. G.C. Anawati, *Op. Cit.*

32. Leo Sweeney, "Doctrine of Creation in *Liber de causis,*" in *An Etienne Gilson Tribute* (Milwaukee, 1959), pp. 274-89; see also Leo Sweeney, "Research Difficulties in the *Liber de causis,*" *The Modern Schoolman* 36 (1959): 109-16.

33. Etienne Gilson, *History of Christian Philosophy in the Middle Ages* (New York, 1955), p. 236.

34. H.D. Saffrey, "L'état. . .," *Op. Cit.,* p. 280.

35. For a discussion of the essential differences between the *Liber* and the *Elements* see H.D. Saffrey's Introduction to Aquinas' commentary on *The Book of Causes, Op. Cit.*

36. See H.D. Saffrey ed. of Aquinas' commentary on the *Liber de causis, Op. Cit.* cf also: G.C. Anawati, "Prolégomènes. . . ," *Op. Cit.,* pp. 135-136.

37. Leo Sweeney, S.J., in "Research Difficulties in the *Liber de causis,*" *Op. Cit.,* signals three obstacles that make research on this opuscule difficult. The first is precisely the complex and subtle use the author of the *De causis* makes of Proclus. The two others are important to note as well. Second, the author attempts to do too much in so short a treatise, that is, to unfold an entire Neo-Platonic universe in all its interrelations. Third, the author is given to occasional inconsistencies.

38. F. Van Steenberghen, *La bibliothèque du philosophe médiévaliste* (Louvain: Publications universitaires, 1974), p. 48.

The Book of Causes

I

1. Every primary cause exercises more influence upon its effect than [does] the universal second cause.[1]
2. Therefore, when the universal second cause removes its power from a thing, the universal prime cause does not withdraw its power from it.
3. This is because the universal prime cause acts upon the effect of the second cause, before the universal second cause that follows the universal prime cause acts upon it [the effect].
4. Therefore, when the second cause, which follows, brings about the effect, its action does not dispense from the prime cause that is above it.
5. And when the second cause separates itself from the effect, which follows it, the prime [cause] that is above the second, since it is cause of the second, does not separate itself from that effect (. . .).[2]
6. And indeed, we may exemplify this by [an analysis of] "being" [*esse*],[3] "living," and "man."
7. This is because a thing must be "being" first of all, then "living," and after "man."
8. For "living" is the proximate cause of "man"; and "being," his remote cause.
9. Consequently, "being" is more intensely the cause of "man" than "living," because it is the cause of "living," which is the cause of "man."
10. And similarly, when you posit "rationality" as the cause of "man," "being" is more intensely the cause of "man" than "rationality," because it is the cause of his cause.

11. And proof of what we say is that, when you remove "rational power" from "man," he does not remain "man" but he does remain "living," "breathing," "sensitive." And when you remove "living" from him, he does not remain "living" but he does remain "being," because "being" is not removed from him, but "living" is removed; since the cause is not removed by the removal of its effect, "man" therefore remains "being." Consequently, when the individual is not "man," it is "animal"; and if not "animal," it is mere "being."

12. Therefore, it is by now manifest and clear that the remote prime cause encompasses more and is more intensely the cause of a thing than its proximate cause.

13. As a result, its operation comes to be a more intense adherence to the thing than the operation of the proximate cause. And this indeed did not come to be like this, except because the thing is first of all under the influence of the remote power and only then under the influence of the power that is under the first.

14. And the prime cause aids the second cause in its operation, since every operation the second cause performs the prime cause also performs; however, it performs it in another manner, higher and more sublime.

15. And when the second cause removes itself from its effect, the prime cause does not remove itself from it, because the prime cause has a greater and more intense adherence to the thing than its proximate cause.

16. And the effect of the second cause holds only through the power of the prime cause.

17. This is because, when the second cause produces a thing, the prime cause that is above the second cause overflows[4] of its own power upon that thing and, consequently, adheres to it with an intense adherence and conserves it.

18. Therefore, it is by now manifest and clear that the remote cause is more intensely the cause of the thing than the proximate cause that follows it, and that the remote cause overflows its power upon the thing and conserves it and does not separate itself from it with the separation of the proximate cause; on the contrary, the remote cause remains in it and adheres to it with an intense adherence, according to what we have shown and exposed.

II

19. Every higher being is either above eternity and before it, or is coexistent with eternity, or is after eternity and beyond time.

20. Indeed, the being that is before eternity is the First Cause, because it is the cause of eternity.

21. And indeed, the being that is coexistent with eternity is Intelligence, because it is the second being, {according to the one and the same disposition,[5] wherefore neither does it suffer [alteration] nor is it destroyed}.

22. Indeed, the being that is after eternity and beyond time is Soul, because it is on the horizon of eternity from below and beyond time.

23. And proof that the First Cause is before eternity itself is that being is acquired in eternity.

24. And I say that all eternity is being, but not all being is eternity. Therefore, being is more common than eternity. And the First Cause is beyond eternity, because eternity is its effect.

25. And Intelligence {is proportionate to or} is commensurate with eternity, because it is coextensive with it; and it is neither changed nor destroyed.

26. And Soul is attached to eternity from below, because it is more susceptible of impression than Intelligence; and it is beyond time, because it is the cause of time.

III

27. Every noble soul has three operations; {for among its works there is} a vital[6] operation, an intellectual operation, and a divine operation.

28. Now its operation is divine because it prepares[7] Nature by the power that is in it from the First Cause.

29. Now its operation is intellectual because it knows things by the power of the Intelligence that is in it.

30. Now its operation is vital because it moves the First Body and all natural bodies, since it is the cause of the movement of bodies and of the operation of Nature.

31. And the soul performs these operations only because it is itself an example of the higher power.

32. This is because the First Cause created the being of Soul by mediation of Intelligence, and as a result Soul has come to perform a divine operation.

33. Therefore, after the First Cause created the being of Soul, it posited Soul as the {substrate}[8] on which Intelligence performs its own operations.

34. As a result then, the intellectual Soul performs an intellectual operation. And since Soul receives the impression of Intelligence,[9] it has come to have a lower operation than Intelligence with respect to its own impression of what is under it.

35. This is because it impresses things only by movement, namely, because what is under it receives its operation only if Soul moves it. For this reason then, it comes to be that Soul moves bodies; for it is a property of Soul to vivify bodies, when it overflows its power upon them; and it directly leads them to a correct operation.[10]

36. Therefore, it is by now manifest that Soul has three operations, because it has three powers: namely, a divine power, the power of Intelligence, and the power of its essence, according to what we have explained and shown.

IV

37. The first of things created is being and nothing has been created before it.[11]

38. This is because being is above sense and above Soul and above Intelligence, and there is after the First Cause nothing more broadly or previously created than it.

39. As a result then, Being has come to be higher than all created things and more intensely unified.

40. And it has come to be such only because of its proximity to the pure, one, and true Being, in which there is no multitude of any kind.

41. And although created being is one it is nevertheless multiple, namely, because it receives multiplicity.

42. And indeed, even though being is simple and there is nothing created more simple than it, it has nevertheless come to be manifold only because it is a composite of finite and infinite.

43. Consequently, all of it[12] that follows the First Cause is *achili,*[13] {that is,} Intelligence, complete and ultimate in power and the other perfections.

44. And the intelligible forms in it are broader and more intensely universal. But the part of it that is lower is likewise Intelligence; however, it is under that Intelligence with respect to plenitude, power, and perfections. And the intelligible forms in it are not as extensive as their amplitude in that Intelligence. And indeed, the First Created Being is totally Intelligence; however, Intelligence in it is diverse in the manner we have indicated.

45. And because Intelligence is diversified, thence the intelligible form becomes diverse. And just as from one form, because it is diversified, there come forth in the world below individuals infinite in multitude; similarly, from the First Created Being, because it is diversified, there appears an infinity of intelligible forms.

46. However, although they are diversified, they are not separated from one another in the same manner as the separation of individuals.

47. This is because they are united without corruption and distinguished without separation, since they are one having a multitude and a multitude in unity.[14]

48. And the First Intelligences overflow upon the Second Intelligences the perfections they receive from the First Cause and extend these perfections in them until they reach the last of them.

(V)

49. The First Higher Intelligences, which follow the First Cause, impress the second, steadfast forms, which are not destroyed such that they must be renewed again. However, the Second Intelligences impress the declining separable forms, such as Soul.

50. For Soul results from the impression of the Second Intelligence that follows lower created being.

51. And Souls become multiple only by the manner in which Intelligences become multiple. This is because the being of Soul is likewise finite, but the part of it that is lower is indefinite.

52. Therefore, the Souls that follow *alachili*, {that is,} Intelligence, are complete, perfect, limited in declination and separation; and the Souls that follow lower being are under the higher Souls with respect to plenitude and declination.

53. And the higher Souls overflow perfections, which they receive from Intelligence, upon the lower Souls.

54. And every Soul that receives more power from Intelligence is stronger with respect to impression; and what is impressed by it is stable, steadfast; and its movement is an equal, continuous movement.[15] And that Soul in which there is less power of Intelligence is under the First Souls with respect to impression; and what is impressed by it is weak, evanescent, destructible.

55. However, although this is so [the impression] remains by virtue of generation.

56. Therefore, it is by now shown why the intelligible forms became manifold, and there is but one, simple being; and why souls became manifold, some of which are stronger than others, and yet their being is one, simple, and has no diversity.

V(VI)

57. The First Cause is above all description. And tongues fail to describe it only because they are unable to describe its being, since the First Cause is above every cause and is described only through the second causes that are illuminated by the light of the First Cause.

58. This is because the First Cause does not cease illuminating its effect but is not itself illuminated by any other light, because it is pure light above which there is no light.

59. Therefore, from this it has come to be that the First [Cause] alone defies description; this is so only because there is no cause above it through which it may be known;

60. for indeed, everything is known and described only through its cause. Therefore, when a thing is a cause only and is not an effect, it is not known through a prime cause; nor is it described, since it is above description; nor does discourse attain it.

61. This is because description[16] only comes to be by means of discourse,[17] and discourse by means of intelligence,[18] and intelligence by means of reasoning,[19] and reasoning by means of imagination,[20] and imagination by means of sense.[21] However, the First Cause is above all things, since it is their cause; as a result then, it comes to be that it does not itself fall under sense or imagination or reasoning or intelligence or discourse; consequently, it is not describable.

62. And I say furthermore that a thing either is sensible and falls under sense; or that it is imaginable and falls under imagination; or that it is stable, steadfast according to one and the same disposition, and is intelligible; or that it is changeable or destructible, subject to generation and corruption, and falls under reasoning. But the First Cause is above the eternal intelligible things and the destructible things, on which account neither sense nor imagination nor reasoning nor intelligence can grasp it.

63. And indeed, the First Cause is signified[22] only by the second cause, which is Intelligence; and it is called by the name of its first effect but only in a higher and better manner, because what belongs to the effect also belongs to the cause, although in a more sublime, better, and more noble manner, as we have shown.

VI(VII)

64. Intelligence is an indivisible substance.

65. This is because, if it is without magnitude and is not a body and does not move, then without doubt it is indivisible.

66. And furthermore, everything divisible is divided only either into multitude or into magnitude or into its movement.

67. Therefore, when a thing exists according to this disposition, it falls under time, because it receives division only in time. And indeed, Intelligence is not situated in time; on the contrary, in eternity; on which account it has come to be higher and superior to every body and to all magnitude. But if multitude is found in it, it is found only as though it were a thing existing as one. Therefore, since Intelligence exists in this manner, it does not receive any division at all.

68. And {indeed,} proof of this is its reversion upon its own essence, namely, because it does not extend itself the way an extended thing does, such that one of its extremities be distant from the other.

69. This is because, when it wants knowledge[23] of a corporeal (. . .)[24] thing, it does not extend[25] itself with the thing; but it remains steadfast according to its disposition, because it is a form through which nothing passes.[26] And indeed, bodies are not like this.

70. And proof (. . .)[27] that Intelligence is not a body and that its substance and its operations do not divide is that both are one and the same thing. And indeed, Intelligence is multiple because of the perfections that come to it from the First Cause. And although it is multiple in this manner, nevertheless, because it is proximate to the One, it comes to be one; and it does not divide. Moreover, Intelligence does not receive division because it is the first effect that was created by the First Cause, and unity is worthier of it than division.

71. Therefore, it is by now verified that Intelligence is a substance that is without magnitude and is not a body and does not move by any of the modes of corporeal movement: on which account it has come to be above time {and in eternity}, as we have shown.

VII(VIII)

72. Every Intelligence knows what is above itself and what is under itself; however, it knows what is under itself because it is its cause, and it knows what is above itself because it acquires its perfections from it.

73. And indeed, Intelligence is an intellectual substance; therefore, after the mode of its own substance it knows the things it acquires from above and the things of which it is the cause.

74. Therefore, it discerns what is above it and what is under it; and it knows that what is above itself is its cause and that what is under itself is caused by it; and it knows its cause and its effect after the mode of its intrinsic cause,[28] namely, after the mode of its own substance.

75. And similarly, every knower knows a better thing and a lower and worse thing only after the mode of its own substance and its own being, not after the mode according to which things are in themselves.

76. And if this is so, then without doubt the perfections that descend from the First Cause upon Intelligence become intelligible in it; and similarly, sensible corporeal things become intelligible in Intelligence.

77. This is because the things that are in Intelligence are not the impressions themselves; on the contrary, they are the causes of the impressions. And proof of this is that Intelligence itself is the cause of the things that are under it inasmuch as it is Intelligence. Therefore, if Intelligence is the cause of things inasmuch as it is Intelligence, then without doubt the causes of things within Intelligence are also intelligible.

78. Therefore, it is by now manifest that the things above Intelligence and those under it are [in Intelligence] by viture of intellectual power; and similarly, that the corporeal things with intelligence are intelligible, and the intelligible things within Intelligence are intelligible, because Intelligence is the cause of the cause of their being; and that because Intelligence apprehends [things] only after the mode of its own substance, and since it is Intelligence, it apprehends things with an intellectual apprehension, whether the things be intelligible or corporeal.

VIII (IX)

79. The stability and essence of every Intelligence is from the Pure Goodness, which is the First Cause.

80. And {indeed,} the power of Intelligence has a stronger unity than the second things that are after it, since they do not reach its knowledge. And it has come to be like this, only because Intelligence is the cause of what is under it.

81. And proof of this is what we are going to recall: Intelligence governs all the things that are under it by virtue of the divine power that is in it; and by that divine power, it maintains things, because by virtue of that same power, it is the cause of things; and it maintains all the things that are under it and contains them.

82. This is because everything that is first with respect to things and is their cause maintains those things and governs them, and nothing of them escapes from it because of its high power. Therefore, Intelligence is the sovereign over the things that are under it; and it maintains them and governs them, just as Nature governs the things that are under it by virtue of the power of Intelligence. And similarly, Intelligence governs Nature by virtue of the divine power.

83. And indeed, Intelligence has come to be that which maintains and governs the things that are after it and that which suspends its own power over them, only because they are not a substantial power for it; {but rather,} it is the power of substantial powers, because it is their cause.

84. And indeed, Intelligence encompasses the things it produces, both Nature and the horizon of Nature, namely, the Soul, for it is above Nature.

85. This is because Nature contains generation and Soul contains Nature and Intelligence contains Soul.

86. Therefore, Intelligence contains all things; and Intelligence has come to be in that position only by virtue of the First Cause, which rises above all things because it is the cause of Intelligence and Soul and Nature and the rest of things.

87. And indeed, the First Cause is neither Intelligence nor Soul nor Nature; on the contrary, it is above {Intelligence and} Soul and Nature, because it creates all things. However, it creates Intelligence without an intermediary and creates Soul and Nature and the rest of things by mediation of Intelligence.

88. And indeed, divine knowledge is not like the knowledge of intellectual beings nor like the knowledge of animated beings; on the contrary, it is above the knowledge of Intelligence and the knowledge of Soul, because it creates these knowledges.

89. And indeed, divine power is above all intellectual and vital and natural power, because it is the cause of all power

90. And Intelligence has *yliathim* [principle of determination][29] because it is being and form; and similarly, Soul has *yliathim;* and Nature has *yliathim.* But indeed, the First Cause does not have *yliathim,* because it is being only.

91. And if anyone says, "The First Cause must have *yliathim,*" we will say, "Its *yliathim* in its infinity and its individuality is Pure Goodness, overflowing every perfection upon Intelligence and upon the rest of things by mediation of Intelligence."

IX (X)

92. Every Intelligence is full of forms; however, among the Intelligences are those that contain less universal forms, and among them are those that contain more universal forms.

93. This is because the forms that are in the Second Lower Intelligences in a particular mode are in the First Intelligences in a universal mode; and the forms that are in the First Intelligences in a universal mode are in the Second Intelligences in a particular mode.

94. And there is a great power in the First Intelligences, because they have a more intense unity than the Second Lower Intelligences; and there are weaker powers in the Second Lower Intelligences, because they have less unity and more multiplicity.

95. This is because the Intelligences that are proximate to the Pure True One are fewer in number and have a greater power; and the Intelligences that are more remote from the Pure True One are more numerous and have a weaker power.

96. And because the Intelligences proximate to the Pure True {One,} are fewer in number and have a greater power, it happens that the forms that proceed from the First Intelligences proceed by a universal unified procession (. . .).[30]

97. And {indeed,} we say in summary that the forms that come from the First Intelligences to the Second have a weaker procession and a stronger separation.

98. On which account, it comes to be that the Second Intelligences turn their gaze upon the universal form, which is in the universal Intelligences, and divide it and separate it, because they cannot receive those forms after the mode of truth and certitude of the latter, but only after the mode according to which they are able to receive them, {namely, through separation and division.

99. And, similarly, everything receives what is above it only after the mode according to which it can receive it}[31] not after the mode according to which the thing received exists.

X (XI)

100. Every Intelligence understands the eternal things that do not perish and do not fall under time.

101. This is because, if Intelligence never moves, then it is the cause of the eternal things that do not perish {or change} and are not subject to generation and corruption. And indeed, Intelligence is like this only because it understands the thing through its own being; and its being is eternal, because it does not corrupt (. . .).[32]

102. Therefore, since this is so, we say that things (. . .)[33] are destructible by reason of corporeity, namely, by reason of a temporal corporeal cause, not by reason of an eternal intelligible cause.

XI (XII)

103. All of the First Things are in one another after the mode according to which it is proper for each to be in the other.[34]

104. For in Being there are life and intelligence, and in Life there are being and intelligence, and in Intelligence there are being and life.

105. However, being and life in Intelligence are two *alachili*, {that is,} Intelligences; and being and intelligence in Life are two lives; and intelligence and life in Being are two beings.

106. And {indeed,} this is so only because every one of the First Things is either a cause or an effect.[35] Therefore, the effect is in the cause after the mode of the cause, and the cause is in the effect after the mode of the effect.

107. And {indeed,} we say in summary that one thing acting upon another after the mode of a cause is in the other only after the mode of the latter,[36] for example: Sense is in Soul in a vital mode, Soul is in Intelligence in an intelligible mode, Intelligence is in Being in an essential mode, First Being is in Intelligence in an intelligible mode, Intelligence is in Soul in a vital mode, and Soul is in Sense in a sensible mode.

108. And let us reiterate and say that Sense is in Soul and Intelligence is in the First Cause after the modes of these latter, according to what we have shown.

XII (XIII)

109. Every Intelligence understands its own essence.

110. This is because it is at the same time what understands and what is understood. Consequently, since Intelligence is both what understands and what is understood, then without doubt it sees its own essence.

111. And, when it sees its own essence, it knows that it understands its own essence by virtue of its own cognitive act.

112. And, when it knows its own essence, it knows the other things that are under it, because they come from it.

113. Nevertheless, they are in it in an intelligible mode. Therefore, Intelligence and the things understood are one.

114. Consequently, if the things understood and Intelligence are one, and if Intelligence knows its own being, then without doubt when it sees its own essence, it knows the other things; and when it knows the other things, it knows its own essence, since when it knows the other things, it knows them only because they are intelligibles. Therefore, Intelligence knows its own essence and it knows the intelligibles simultaneously, as we have shown.

XIII (XIV)

115. In every Soul there are sensible things inasmuch as it is their exemplar; and in each there are intelligible things, because it knows them.

116. And Soul has come to be like this only because it is the bridge[37] between the intelligible things that do not move and the sensible things that are moved.

117. And since Soul is like this, it comes to be that it impresses corporeal things, on which account it has come to be the cause of bodies and the effect of the Intelligence that is before it.

118. Therefore, the things that are impressed by Soul are [present] in Soul by virtue of an exemplary intention, namely, because sensible things are reproduced following the exemplar of Soul; but the things that are above Soul are in it in an acquired mode.

119. Therefore, since this is so, let us reiterate and say that all sensible things are in Soul after the mode of a cause, on which account Soul is their exemplary cause.

120. And I understand by "Soul" the power that makes sensible things;

121. however, the efficient power in Soul is not material, and the corporeal power in Soul is spiritual, and the power that impresses things having dimensions is itself without dimension.

122. However, intelligible things are in Soul in an accidental mode, namely, because intelligible things that do not divide are in Soul in a divisible mode. Therefore, unified intelligible things are in Soul after a mode that is multiple, and intelligible things that do not move are in Soul after a mode of movement.

123. Therefore, it has already been shown that(. . .)[38] intelligible and sensible things are in Soul; however, sensible, corporeal, mobile things are in Soul in a vital, spiritual, unified mode; but intelligible, unified, quiescent things are in Soul after a mode that is multiple according to movement (. . .).[39]

XIV (XV)

124. Every knower that knows its own essence reverts upon its own essence with a complete reversion.

125. This is because knowledge is but an intelligible action. Therefore, when the knower knows its own essence, it then reverts upon its own essence by virtue of its own intelligible operation.

126. And this is so only because the knower and the known are one thing, since the knowledge the knower has of its own essence [moves] from itself and to itself: it [proceeds] from itself because it is the knower, and it [reverts] to itself because it is the known.

127. This is because, by the fact that the knowledge is the knowledge of the knower, and that the knower knows its own essence, its operation reverts upon its own essence; consequently, its substance likewise reverts upon its own essence.

128. And by "reversion of the substance upon its own essence," I mean only that it is subsistent, stable in itself, not in need of a support for its stability and its essence, because it is a simple, self-sufficient substance.

XV (XVI)

129. All infinite powers depend from the First Infinite, which is the Power of powers, not because it is acquired, steadfast, subsistent in existent things [*entibus*]; on the contrary, it is the power that belongs to existent things having stability.

130. And if anyone should say that the First Created Being [*ens*], namely, Intelligence, is an Infinite Power, we would say that created being [*ens*] is not a Power; on the contrary, a certain power belongs to it.

131. And indeed, its power has come to be infinite only from below, not from above, because it is not the pure Power that is a power only because it is Power and is the thing that is finite neither from below nor from above. However, the First Created Being, namely, Intelligence, is finite; and its power is finite (. . .)[40] by the fact that its cause remains.

132. However, the First Creative Being [*ens*] is the First Pure Infinite.

133. Consequently, if the powerful beings [*entia*]are infinite because of their acquisition [of infinitude] from the First Pure Infinite, as a result of which they are beings [*entia*], and if the First Being itself is what posits the infinite things, then without doubt it is above the infinite.

134. However, the First Created Being, namely, Intelligence, is not infinite; on the contrary, it is said that it is infinite; but it is not said that it is that which is the Infinite itself.[41]

135. Therefore, the First Being is the measure of the first intelligible beings and of the second sensible beings, namely, because it is what created beings and measured them by a measure suitable to each being.

136. Therefore, let us reiterate and say that the First Creative Being is above the infinite; but the second created being is [not][42] infinite; and what is between the First Creative Being and the second created being in infinite.

137. And the other simple perfections, such as life and light and those that are similar to them, are the causes of all things that have these perfections, namely, because the infinite comes from the First Cause; and the first effect is the cause of all life and similarly of the other perfections that descend from the First Cause first of all upon the first effect — and it is Intelligence — and then upon the other intelligible and corporeal effects, by mediation of Intelligence.

XVI (XVII)

138. Every unified power is more infinite than a multiple power.

139. This is because the First Infinite, which is Intelligence, is proxi-

mate to the Pure True One. As a result then, it has come to be that in every power proximate to the (. . .)[43] True One there is more infinity than in the power remote from it.

140. This is because, when power begins to become multiple, then its unity is destroyed; and when its unity is destroyed, its infinity is destroyed. And its infinity is destroyed only because it is divided.

141. And proof of this is that, when a divided power comes together more and is more unified, it increases and becomes stronger and performs wondrous operations; and, when it is more separated and more divided, it decreases and is weakened and performs base operations.

142. Therefore, it is by now manifest and clear that the more power approaches the Pure True One, the more intense becomes its unity; and to the extent that its unity becomes more intense, its infinity becomes more apparent and more manifest, and its operations are great, wondrous, and noble operations.

XVII (XVIII)

143. All things [are] beings [*entia*] because of the First Being, all things are self-moving because of the First Life, and all intelligible things have knowledge because of the First Intelligence.

144. This is because, if every cause gives something [of itself] to its effect, then without doubt the First Being gives being [*ens*] to all effects.

145. And similarly, Life gives movement to its effects, because life is a procession that proceeds from the quiescent, eternal First Being, and [it is] the first movement.

146. And similarly, Intelligence gives knowledge to its effects.

147. This is because all true knowledge exists only because of Intelligence; and Intelligence is the first knower that is, and it overflows knowledge upon the other knowers.

148. However, let us reiterate and say that the First Being is quiescent and is the cause of causes; and, if it gives being to all things, then it gives [being] to them after the mode of creation. However, the First Life gives life to those that are under it not after the mode of creation, but rather after the mode of a form. And similarly, Intelligence gives knowledge and the other things to those that are under it only after the mode of a form (. . .).[44]

XVIII (XIX)

149. Among the Intelligences, there is that which is the divine Intelligence, because it receives by means of a manifold reception those of the first perfections that proceed from the First Cause. And among them, there is that which is mere Intelligence, because it receives of the first perfections only by mediation of the First Intelligence. And among the Souls, there is that which is the intelligible Soul, because it depends from Intelligence; and among them, there is that which is mere Soul. And among the Natural Bodies, there is that which has a Soul governing and directing it; and among them, there are those that are mere Natural Bodies, which do not have souls.

150. And this does not come to be like this, except because it is itself (. . .)[45] and it is not all intellectual nor all vital nor all corporeal, nor does it depend from the cause that is above it; only the part of it that is complete and perfect depends from the cause that is above it,

151. namely, because not every Intelligence depends from the perfections of the First Cause, but only the Intelligence that is first of all complete and perfect. For it is able to receive the perfections that descend from the First Cause and to depend from them on account of the intensity of its unity.[46]

152. And similarly, not every Soul depends from Intelligence, but only the Soul that is complete, perfect, and more intensely united with Intelligence, inasmuch as it depends from the Intelligence that is complete Intelligence.

153. And similarly, not every Body has a Soul, but only the Body that is complete and perfect, as though it were rational.

154. And the other intelligible degrees follow this pattern (. . .).[47]

XIX (XX)

155. The First Cause governs all things without intermingling with them.

156. This is because its governance does not weaken or destroy its unity, which is exalted above everything; nor does the essence of its unity, although separated from things, prevent it from governing them.

157. This is because the First Cause is stable, perpetually steadfast with its pure unity; it governs all created things; and it overflows upon them the power of life and perfections according to the mode of the power and the capacity {of these things that are receptive}. For the First Goodness overflows perfections upon all things with one effluence; however, each individual thing receives of that effluence after the mode of its own power and being.

158. And the First Goodness overflows perfections upon all things only through one mode, because it is Goodness merely through its own *esse*[48] and *ens*[49] and power, just because it is goodness; and goodness {and power} and being are one and the same thing. Therefore, insasmuch as the First Being and Goodness are but one thing, it comes to be that it overflows perfections upon things with one common effluence (. . .).[50] But the perfections and gifts are diversified by the concurrence of the recipient. This is because those that receive perfections do not receive [them] equally; on the contrary, some of them receive more than others, and this is because of the magnitude of their abundance.

159. Therefore, let us reiterate and say that between every agent, which acts through its being alone, and its product there is no connecting link [*continuator*] or any other intermediary thing. But there is a connecting link between the agent and its product only by reason of an addition to being, namely, when the agent and its product are [linked] by virute of an instrument and when [the agent] does not act by means of its being (. . .);[51] and they are composed. On which account, the recipient receives by means of the continuity between itself and its producer, and the agent that produces this product is separate from its product (. . .).[52]

160. But the agent that has no connecting link at all between itself and its product is a true agent and a true governor, which makes things by maximum of beauty, [that beauty] beyond which no other beauty is possible; and it governs its product by the maximum of governance.

161. This is because it governs things after the mode through which it acts, and it acts only through its own Being [*ens*]; therefore, its Being [*ens*] likewise will be its governance. On which account it comes to be that it governs and acts by the maximum of beauty and governance, in which there is neither diversity nor tortuosity.

And the operations and governance due to the prime causes are diversified only in accordance with the merit of the recipient.

XX (XXI)

162. The First [Cause] is richness *per se,* and there is no greater richness.
163. And proof of this is its unity, for its unity is not dispersed in it; on the contrary, its unity is pure, because it is simple in the maximum of simplicity.
164. However, if anyone wants to know that the First [Cause] is this richness, let him turn his mind toward composite things and inquire about them with an investigative inquiry. For he will find every composite diminished, indeed, needing either another or the things of which it is composed. However, the simple thing,(. . .)[53] the One that is Goodness, is one; its unity is its goodness; and (. . .)[54] its goodness is one and the same thing.
165. Therefore, that thing is the greater richness that overflows without an effluence coming to be upon it in any manner. However, the other intelligible or corporeal things are not rich *per se;* on the contrary, they need the true One overflowing upon them perfections and all good things.

XXI (XXII)

166. The First Cause is above every name by which it is named.
167. For neither diminution nor plenitude alone pertain to it; because the diminution is not complete, and it cannot perform a complete operation when it is diminished. And "complete" from our viewpoint, although it is self-sufficient, it nevertheless cannot create anything else or overflow of itself anything at all.
168. Therefore, if this is so {from our viewpoint}, then we say that the First [Cause] is neither diminished nor complete only; on the contrary, it is above the complete,
169. because it creates things and overflows perfections upon them with complete effluence, because it is Goodness that has neither end nor limits.
170. Therefore, the First Goodness fills all worlds with perfections; however, every world receives of that perfection only after the mode of its potency.

171. Therefore, it is by now shown and manifest that the First Cause is above every name by which it is named and is superior to it and higher.

XXII (XXIII)

172. Every divine Intelligence knows things inasmuch as it is an Intelligence, and it governs them inasmuch as it is divine.
173. This is because the property of Intelligence is knowledge, and its plenitude and perfection is [given] only so that it may be a knower. Therefore, God, the blessed and sublime, governs, because he fills things with perfections. And Intelligence is the first thing created and is more like the sublime God; and as a consequence, Intelligence governs the things that are under it. And, just as God, the blessed and most high, overflows perfections upon things, similarly Intelligence overflows knowledge upon the things that are under it.
174. However, although Intelligence governs the things that are under it, nevertheless God, the blessed and sublime, precedes Intelligence with respect to governance; and he governs things with a more sublime and higher order of governance than that of Intelligence, because it is he that gives Intelligence its governance.
175. And proof of this is that the things that do (not) receive the governance of Intelligence receive the governance of the Creator of Intelligence; this is because nothing at all escapes his governance, since he wills it to happen that all things {simultaneously} receive his perfections.
This is because not all things desire Intelligence or desire to receive it; but all things both desire the perfections of the First [Cause] and desire to receive it with a manifold desire. And of this there is no one that doubts.

XXIII (XXIV)

176. The First Cause exists in all things according to one and the same disposition, but all things do not exist in the First Cause according to one and the same disposition.
177. This is because, although the First Cause exists in all things, every single thing however receives it according to the mode of its potency.

178. And this is because among things there are those that receive the First Cause by a unified reception and those that receive it by a multiplied reception; and among them are those that receive it by an eternal reception and those that receive it by a temporal reception; and among them are those that receive it by a spiritual reception and those that receive it by a corporeal reception.

179. And indeed, the diversity of reception comes not from the First Cause but from the recipient. For the one receiving is diversified; therefore, as a result what is received is diversified. But the one overflowing, existing as one not diverse, overflows perfections equally upon all things; for perfections overflow from the First Cause equally upon all things. Therefore, things are the cause of the diversity in the effluence of perfections upon things. Therefore, without doubt all things are not found in the First Cause in one and the same mode. Moreoever, it is by now shown that the First Cause is found in all things in one and the same mode, but that all things are not found in it in one and the same mode.

180. Therefore, to the extent of its proximity to the First Cause and to the extent of its capacity to receive it, to that extent a thing is able to receive of the First Cause and to take delight in it. This is because the thing receives of the First Cause and takes delight in it only after the mode of its own being. And by "being" I mean only "knowledge," for to the extent that the thing knows the First Creative Cause to that extent it receives of it and takes delight in it, as we have shown.

XXIV (XXV)

181. {Intelligible unified substances are not generated from another thing.}[55] Every substance subsistent by virtue of its own essence is not generated by another thing.

182. And if anyone should say, "It is possible that it be generated from another thing," we would say, "If it is possible that a substance subsistent by virtue of its own essence be generated from another thing, then without doubt that substance is diminished, needing that of which it is generated to complete it."

183. And proof of this is generation itself.

184. For generation is but the path from diminution to plenitude. For, if a thing is found not needing in its generation, namely, in its form and its formation, anything other than itself and it is the cause of its own formation and plenitude, [then] it is complete and perpetually perfect.

185. And it becomes the cause of its own formation and plenitude only because of its perpetual relation to its own cause. Therefore, that relationship is its formation and its very own plenitude.

186. Therefore, it is by now manifest that every substance subsistent by virtue of its essence is not generated from another thing.

XXV (XXVI)

187. Every self-subsistent substance is not subject to corruption.

188. However, if anyone should say, "It is possible that a self-subsistent subtance be subject to corruption," we would say, "If it is possible that a self-subsistent substance be subject to corruption, [then] it is possible that it be separate from its essence and [yet] be stable, subsistent by virtue of its own essence [but] without its own essence." And this is incongruous and impossible; for, since it is one, simple, and not composite, it is simultaneously its own cause and effect. However, everything subject to corruption becomes corrupt only because of its separation from its cause; but while a thing remains depending from its cause, which maintains and conserves it, it neither perishes nor is it destroyed. Therefore, if this is so, a self-subsistent substance never separates from its cause, because it is inseparable from its essence, since its cause is itself in its self-formation.

189. And it becomes its very own cause only because of its own relation to its own cause; and that relation is its formation. And therefore, because it is perpetually related to its cause and it is the cause of that relation, it is its very own cause in the manner we have indicated, and it neither perishes nor is it destroyed, because it is simultaneously its own cause and effect, as we have just shown.

190. Therefore, it is by now verified that every self-subsistent substance neither is destroyed nor does it corrupt.

XXVI (XXVII)

191. Every destructible non-eternal substance is either composed or supported by another thing.

192. Consequently, such substance either needs the things of which it is the composite — and it is composed from them — or it needs a support for its stability and its essence. Therefore, when its support separates from it, it corrupts and is destroyed.

193. But, if the substance is neither composed nor supported, then it is simple and perpetual, and it is neither destroyed nor is it diminished at all.

XXVII (XXVIII)

194. Every substance subsistent by virtue of its own essence is simple and does not divide.

195. And if anyone says, "It is possible that it divide," we will say; "If it is possible that a self-subsistent substance divide and [yet] itself remain simple, it is possible that the essence of a part in its essence be also the essence of a whole. Therefore, if that is possible, the part would revert upon itself, and every part of it would revert upon itself, like the reversion of the whole upon its essence; but this is impossible. Therefore, if this is impossible, a self-subsistent substance is indivisible and simple,"

196. However, if it is not simple but a composite, a part of it would be the better part and another part, the baser part; therefore, the better thing would be made from the baser, and the baser thing, from the better, when every part of it is separate from every other part.

197. Consequently, its totality would not be self-sufficient, since it would need its own parts of which it is the composite. And indeed, this is not the nature of a simple thing, but rather of composite substances.

198. Therefore, it is by now established that every substance subsistent by virtue of its own essence is simple and does not divide; and, when it does not receive division and is simple, it does not receive either corruption or destruction.

XXVIII (XXIX)

199. Every {simple} substance is self-subsistent, namely subsistent by virtue of it own essence {.}

200. {For it} is created outside of time and in its substantiality it is superior to temporal substances.

201. And proof of this is that it is not generated from anything, because it is self-sufficient by virtue of its own essence; and substances generated from something are composite substances that are subject to generation.

202. Therefore, it is by now manifest that every substance subsistent by virtue of its own essence is only [created] outside of time, and that it is higher and superior to time and temporal things.

XXIX (XXX)

203. Every substance created in time either is perpetually in time, and time does not separate itself from it, because it and time were created equally; or it is separated from time, and time is separated from it, because it was created in a certain moment of time.

204. This is because, if created things follow one another,[56] and if the higher substance is followed only by a substance similar to it, not by a substance dissimilar to it, [then] the substances similar to the higher substances — and they are the created substances from which time does not separate itself — come before the substances that do (not) resemble the eternal substances — and they are the substances cut from time, created in certain moments of time. Therefore, it is not possible that the substances created in certain moments of time be continuous with the eternal substances, because they do not resemble them at all. Therefore, the substances eternal in time are those that are continuous with the eternal substances, and they are intermediaries between the stable substances and the substances cut out of time. And it is not possible that the eternal substances that are above time follow the temporal substances created in time, except by mediation of the temporal substances eternal in time.

205. And indeed, these substances have come to be intermediaries, only because they share with the sublime substances in permanence, and they share in the temporal substances cut out of time by reason of generation; for although they are eternal, their permanence nevertheless comes by virtue of generation and movement.

206. And the eternal substances coexistent with time are similar to the eternal substances that are above time through durability, but they do not resemble them in movement and generation.

Morever, the substances cut out of time do not resemble the eternal substances that are above time in any manner. Therefore, if they do not resemble them, they are then unable to receive them or to touch them. Consequently, there must be substances that touch the eternal substances that are above time, and they are those that touch the substances cut out of time.

207. Therefore, they will unite by their movement the substances cut out of time and the eternal substances that are above time. And they will unite by their durability the substances that are above time and the substances that are under time, namely, those that are subject to generation and corruption. And they will unite the perfect substances and the base substances, so that the base substances might not be deprived of the perfect substances and [thereby] deprived of all perfections and harmony and be without continuity or stability.

208. Therefore, from this it is by now shown that there are two kinds of durability, one of which is eternal; the other, temporal. However, one of the two durabilities is stable and quiescent, the other is mobile; and one of them is unified and all its operations [are] simultaneous — certain ones are not before certain others — and the other is flowing and extended — certain of its operations are before certain others. And the totality of one of them exists by virtue of its own essence; and the totality of the other exists by virtue of its own parts, each of which is separated from its own counterpart after the mode of a prior and a posterior.

209. Therefore, it is by now manifest that certain of the substances are ones that are eternal above time; and [certain] of them are eternal equal to time, and time does not separate itself from them; and [certain] of them are ones that have been cut out of time, and time separates itself from the higher and the lower [part] of them, {namely, from their beginning and their end} and they are the substances that are subject to generation and corruption.

XXX (XXXI)

210. Between the thing whose substance and action are in the limit of eternity and the thing whose substance and action are in the limit of time, there is an intermediary; and it is that whose

substance is in the limit of eternity and whose action is in the limit of time.

211. This is because the thing whose substance falls under time, namely, because time contains it, falls under time in all its dispositions, wherefore its action also falls under time: because, when the substance of the thing falls under time, without doubt its action also falls under time. Moreover, the thing that falls under time in all its dispositions is separated from the thing that falls under eternity in all its dispositions. Furthermore, there is continuity only among similar things. Therefore, between the two, there must be another, third, intermediary thing whose substance falls under eternity and whose operation falls under time.

212. For it is impossible that there be a thing whose substance falls under time and whose action falls under eternity: for thus its action would be better than its substance; however, this is impossible.[57]

213. Therefore, it is manifest that, between the things that fall under time by reason of both their substances and their actions and those that fall under the limit of eternity, there are those things that fall both under eternity by reason of their substances and under time by reason of their operations, as we have shown.

XXXI (XXXII)

214. Every substance that falls under eternity in certain of its dispositions and under time in certain other of its dispositions is simultaneously being [*ens*] and generation.[58]

215. For {every} thing that falls under eternity is truly being, and every thing that falls under time is truly generation. Therefore, if this is so and if one and the same thing falls under both eternity and time, then it is both being and generation not by reason of one mode but by different modes.

216. Therefore, it is by now manifest from what we have indicated, that every generated thing that falls under time by reason of its substance has its substance depending from the pure Being, which is the cause of durability and the cause of all eternal and destructible things.

217. There must be a "One" that causes unities to be attained and is not itself attained, but all others are acquired unities.

218. And indeed, proof of this is what I say: if a "One" is found that causes the acquisition [of unities] and is not itself acquired, then what difference [is there] between it and the first [One] that causes the acquisition [of unities]? For it is only possible that either it be similar to it in all dispositions or that there be a difference between the two. Therefore, if it is similar to it in all its dispositions (. . .)[59] then one of them is not first and the other second. But if one of them is not similar to the other in all its dispositions, then without doubt one of them is first and the other second. Therefore, that in which there is a stable unity not obtained from another is the first true One, as we have shown; and that in which there is a unity obtained from another exists [but] in addition to the first true One. If it comes from another then, it is a unity acquired from the first One. Therefore, from this it happens that the pure true One and the other "Ones" are similarly unities; and there is unity only because of the true One, which is the cause of unity.

219. Therefore, it is by now manifest and clear that every unity after the true One is acquired and created; however, the Pure True One creates unities, causing the acquisition [of unities], but is not itself acquired, as we have shown.

Notes

1. For a comparison with Plato's conception of the distinction between primary and secondary or cooperative causes and on the importance of studying primary causes first, see *Timaeus,* 46 d-e.

2. (...) = *a:* The First Cause, therefore, acts more intensely as cause upon a thing than the proximate cause that follows it.

   In translating aphorisms 3, 4, and 5, I have conformed to the sense and punctuation of Fr. Pattin's Latin text, which he considers an improvement upon the Arabic. According to Fr. Pattin, the Arabic text is less correct than his amended Latin, because the Arabic text involes a manifest contradiction, affirming on the one hand that "the universal second cause follows the effect;" and on the other, that "the second cause separates from the effect that follows it." Fr. Pattin's reading of the Arabic, however, is disputed by Richard C. Taylor in "A Note on Chapter 1 of the *Liber de causis,*" *Manuscripta* 22 (1978): 169-72. Taylor explains that the contradiction that Pattin finds is a result of Gerard of Cremona's mistranslation of the Arabic word *"waliya"* as *"sequor"* = "to follow." In the context of *The Book of Causes,* however, *"waliya"* conveys the meaning "to be adjacent to" rather than "to follow." If properly translated, as the following rendering of the Arabic by Taylor shows, the apparent contradiction evaporates: "And this is because the universal first cause acts on the effect of the second cause before the universal second cause which is (immediately) adjacent to it [the effect] acts on it [the effect]. And when the second cause which is adjacent to the effect acts, its action [the action of the second cause] cannot do without the first cause which is above it [the second cause]. And when the second cause separates from the effect which is adjacent to it [the second cause], the first cause which is above it [the second cause] does not separate from it [the effect] because it [the first cause] is the cause of its [the effect's] cause."

3. *esse* = *anniyya*. Gerard of Cremona uses *"esse"* to render the Arabic philosophical word *"anniyya,"* one of the two words used in the Arabic text for being. The other is *"huwiyya,"* which Gerard renders as *"ens."* Richard C. Taylor explains the meaning of this word in the *Liber, "anniyya* . . . is the formal substrate on the basis of which further perfection such as life and intelligence are received. In the *De causis,* there is no notion of being as the act of existence . . .," "St. Thomas and the *Liber de causis* on the Hylmorphic Composition of Separate Substances," *Mediaeval Studies* 41 (1979): 506. On *anniyya* see Marie-Thérèse d'Alverny, *"Anniyya-Anitas,"* in *Mélanges offerts à Etienne Gilson* (Toronto: Pontifical Institute of Mediaeval Studies; Paris: Vrin, 1959), pp. 59-91; R.M. Frank, "The Origin of the Arabic Philosophical Term *Anniyah," Cahiers de Byrsa* 6 (1956): 181-201.

   In the present translation, "being" serves to render both *esse* and *ens.* Whenever "being" translates *"ens,"* it is so indicated in the body of the text the first time it appears in a given context. If no indication is given, "being" is the translation of *esse."* This is consonant with the findings of Taylor, op. cit. and others, such as Leo Sweeney, S.J. who has written: "Throughout the treatise *ens, esse,* and *essentia* all seem to be synonymous," "Doctrine of Creation in *Liber de causis,"* in *An Etienne Gilson Tribute,* ed. Charles J. O'Neil (Milwaukee: Marquette University Press, 1959), p. 280.

4. *influit* = overflows, flows over into. *a: répand; b: ausströmen;* the Arabic text: *afâdat* = emanates. In view of the theistic doctrine of creation professed by the *Liber,* "emanates" is perhaps too misleading a translation. On *fluere, influere,* and *flux* see Leo Sweeney, S.J., *"Esse Primum Creatum* in Albert the Great's *Liber de causis et processu universitatis," The Thomist* 44 (1980): 609-13. On the doctrine of creation in *The Book of Causes* see Sweeney, "The Doctrine of Creation in the *Liber de causis,"* op. cit.; K. Kremer, "Die *Creatio* nach Thomas von Aquin und dem *Liber de causis,"* in *Ekklesia. Festschrift für Bischof Dr. Matthias Wehr* (Trier, 1962), pp. 321-44.

5. *secundum habitudinem unam: p: eodem modo et uniformiter* = in the same manner and uniformly.

6. *animalis* = vital or animated. The substantive is not *animal, -alis* = animal, but *anima, -ae* = soul; hence, a "besouled" operation, not an "animal" operation. See Adriaan Pattin, O.M.I., "Notes sur le vocabulaire philosophique médiévale," *Revue de l'Université d'Ottawa* 33 (1963): 209*.

7. Causality in Neo-Platonism is not, as it is in Aristotelianism, to educe act from potency; rather, it is to imprint, impress, or give an act to another. In book one, chapter ten of the *Sufficientia,* Avicenna says that sub-lunary entities do not strictly-speaking cause; they only *prepare* for the cause. See Patrick Lee, "St. Thomas and Avicenna on the Agent Intellect," *The Thomist* 45 (1981): 46.

8. *stramentum* = literally: that which is strewn down, straw. Therefore, following *b: dem Substrate* = substrate. *a: (instrumentum)* = instrument.

9. Soul, therefore, has a derived intelligence.

10. *et directe producit ea ad operationem rectam: p* observes that this seems to be in contradistinction to what Proclus calls a "cyclic activity." See *d* Proposition 33: "All that proceeds from any principle and reverts upon it has a cyclic activity."

11. On Albert the Great's understanding of *esse* as what is created first, see Leo Sweeney, S.J., *"Esse Primum Creatum* in Albert the Great's *Liber de causis et processu universitatis,* op. cit.; and "The Meaning of *Esse* in Albert the Great's Texts on Creation in *Summa de creaturis* and *Scripta super sententias," Southwestern Journal of Philosophy* 10 (1979): 65-95.

12. *omne quod ex eo* = "all of it," that is, every Intelligence that is a member of this grade of Higher Being. Confer St. Thomas Aquinas, *Expositio super librum De causis,* ed. Saffrey, IV: "Finally, when he says, 'This is: because all . . .,' he shows the difference between the members of this division, namely, between the manifold intelligences."

13. *achili* = *'aql.* See A.M. Goichon, *Lexique de la langue philosophique d'Ibn Sina* (Paris: Desclée de Brouwer, 1938), p. 226, no. 439.

14. We learn from aphorism 42 that there is composition in the Intelligible World. This composition accounts for the diversity of intelligible forms, etc. (aphorism 44). There is, however, a difference in the kind of composition/diversity in the material, sensible world and in the Intelligible World. The Intelligible Universe has only formal distinction and specification, not numeric distinction or local dispersion. There is heterogeneity but not exteriority. The forms can be resolved into their elements and relations, but not divided into parts.

15. *motus aequalis, continuus* = *a:* a circular movement.

16. *narratio* = description: *a: description; b: Bezeichnung.*

17. *loquela* = discourse, or simply speech. *a: parole; b: Sprechen;* the Arabic text: *mantiq.* Confer *d* Proposition 123: λόγος.

    For a comprehensive and schematic expose of this word as well as those given in notes 18-21 below see *S. Thomae Aquinatis in Librum de causis expositio,* ed. Marietti, pp. 48-9.

18. *intelligentia* = intelligence, that is, the act of understanding, intellection. *a: intelligence; b: Erkennnen;* the Arabic text: *alayha.* Confer *d* Proposition 123: γόησις.

19. *cogitatio* = reasoning, that is, discursive thinking or ratiocination. *a: cognition (raisonnement); b: Denken;* the Arabic text: *fikr.* Confer *d* Proposition 123: διάνοια.

20. *meditatio* = imagination, or phantasy. *a: imagination; b: Vorstellung;* the Arabic text: *wahm.* Confer *d* Proposition 123: δόξα.

21. *sensus* = sense, or sensation. *a: sens; b: Sinnenwahrnehmung.* Confer *d* Proposition 123: αἴσθησις.

22. *significatur* = is signified, in contradistinction to *cognoscitur* = is known. The distinction being made here is fundamental to "negative theology." Because the First Cause is absolutely transdecent, it cannot be known or described. However, since Intelligence is the first effect created by the First Cause, and since it most resembles its cause, it alone is capable of "signing" for its cause.

23. *scientiam* = knowledge, in the strict and narrow sense of certain knowledge or science.

24. (...) = *a* and *b:* extended

25. In the Intelligible Universe, there is neither local distance, extension, nor exteriority as there is in the sensible universe. The Intelligences are formally diverse and other; they can be resolved into their elements, but not divided into parts. When they appropriate the form of a corporeal thing, they do so without the condition that results from sensible matter, that is, extension, having parts outside of parts.

26. In contradistinction to Plato, for whom the form passes and is diminished, Plotinus and the Neo-Platonists hold that the form does not pass and is not diminished. Confer *Ennead* VI 5, 8 (15-22).

27. (...) = *a:* as well; *b:* furthermore

28. *per modum qui est causa eius* = literally: after the mode that is the cause of it [i.e., of that knowledge]. Now Intelligence knows by virtue of its own substance, and it is self-constituted by virtue of its own essence, which is its intrinsic cause. Hence, its intrinsic cause is the cause of both its being and its knowledge.

29. *yliathim* = principle of determination. On *yliathim* see Richard C. Taylor, "St. Thomas and the *Liber de causis* on the Hylomorphic Composition of Separate Substances," op. cit. While the other Arabic word in the text, *achili*, is accompanied by the translation *intelligentia*, *yliathim* is left untranslated. There have been numerous attempts to render this concept correctly. Some, following Aquinas, have interpreted it as rooted in the Greek ὕλη = matter as meaning "material principle." Taylor, however, has demonstrated that *yliathim* is Gerard of Cremona's transliteration of the Arabic word *hilyah*, which "far from being derived from the Greek ὕλη and meaning 'matter' or 'material principle' as St. Thomas thought, can be translated as 'ornament,' 'attribute,' 'quality,' 'state,' 'condition,' 'appearance,' and even 'form'" (p. 510). Hence, *yliathim* is the form that limits a thing, or the principle of determination. Confer *a:* Intelligence has a universality because it is being and form; *b:* Intelligence is something complete (a composite) . . .

30. (...) = *a* and *b:* and proceeds from the second Intelligences by a singular dispersed procession

31. The theme of "reception according to the capacity of the recipient" is a frequent one in the *Liber,* e.g., aphorisms 106, 149, 157-58, 161, 170, 177, and 179. This doctrine also plays an important role in Plotinian ontology, see A.H. Armstrong, *The Architecture of the Intelligible Universe in the Philosophy of Plotinus: An Analytical and Historical Study* (Cambridge: Cambridge University Press, 1940); Jonathon Scott Lee, "The Doctrine of Reception According to the Capacity of the Recipient in *Ennead* VI.4-5," *Dionysius* 3 (1979): 79-97, According to Lee, in Plotinus we find a strong reaction against the doctrine of emanation which we find in Plato. Emanation teaches that the idea passes and is weakened in its descent toward plurality and corporeity (see above aphorism 69 and note 26). In place of this doctrine, Plotinus substitutes the doctrine of the integral omnipresence of Being to the sensible world (= eidetic causation), which he supplements with the doctrines of undiminished giving and the limitation of the *eide* by the capacity of the recipient.

32. (...) = *a:* or change

33. (...) = *a:* that are subject to corruption and generation

34. Confer Proclus Proposition 103 *d:* "All things are in all things, but each according to its proper nature."

35. i.e., is [simultaneously] both cause and effect. Confer Plotinus *Ennead* VI [38] 7, 2 (31-35).

36. *per modum quo est causa eius* = *a* and *b:* the thing that is found in another under the form of cause is found there only according to the mode through which [the latter] is found. Confer aphorism 74 above.

37. *expansa* = bridge. Confer *a:* intermediary. The point is that Soul has contact with both intelligibles and sensibles, precisely because it is the horizon between the intelligible world and the sensible world.

38. (...) = *a:* all things, both intelligible and sensible

39. (...) = *a:* as we have shown

40. (...) = *a:* and *b:* likewise

41. *neque dicitur quod est ipsummet quod est non finitum* = literally: and it is not said that it is its very self that is not finite.

42. *sed ens secundum creatum est infinitum: p:* "Sans doubte faut-il corriger le texte latin en: *'est non infinitum'.*"

43. (...) = *a* and *b:* Pure

44. (...) = *a* and *b:* not after the mode of creation because the mode of creation is for the First Cause only

45. (...) = Pattin, following Bardenhewer, calls attention to this defective passage; lacunae exist in both the Arabic and Latin manuscripts. For the sense of the passage, confer Proclus *d* Propositions 110 and 111.

46. *ut vehemens fiat sua unitas* = *a:* because of the force of its unity.

47. (...) = *a:* standard; *b:* analogy

48. *esse* = *anniyya*

49. *ens* = *huwiyya*

50. (...) = *a:* It does not overflow upon some things more than upon others.

51. (...) = *a:* and by certain of its attributes.

52. (...) = *a:* and it does not govern it in any true and proper manner

53. (...) = *a:* and *b:* namely,

54. (...) = *a* and *b:* the One and

55. This first sentence of aphorism 181 does not appear in the body of the Arabic text, but does appear as a marginal note.

56. *sequuntur se ad invicem* = follow one another, that is, if there is continuity and succession between them

57. Confer Proclus Proposition 16 *d:* "For if there were any body whatsoever from which it was inseparable, it could have no activity separable from the body, since it is impossible that if the existence be inseparable from bodies the activity, which proceeds from the existence, should be separable: if so, the activity would be superior to the existence . . ."

   Aphorism 212 seems to be the immediate source of an important objection, raised by Siger of Brabant and others, against two key doctrines of Thomistic anthropology: the powers of the soul and the intellective soul as the form of man's body. Aquinas cites this argument against his position in *De unitate intellectus,* ¶84: "The power of the soul cannot be more immaterial or more simple than the essence of the soul."

58. *ens et generatio* = being and generation. Confer Proclus *d* Proposition 107: "All that is eternal in one regard and temporal in another is at once a Being and a coming-to-be."

59. (...) = *a:* and if it is ONE like it; *b:* and it is likewise a One like that

Bibliography

[ALBERT THE GREAT]. *B. Alberti Magni . . . opera omnia, cura ac labore Augusti Borgnet.* 38 vols. Paris: Vives, 1890-99. Vol. 10 *"Liber de causis et processu universitatis,"* pp. 361-619.

ALONSO, Manuel. "La 'al-anniyya' de Avicena y el problema de la esencia y existencia." *Pensiamento* 14 (1958): 311-46.

ALONSO, Manuel. "Las fuentes literarias del *Liber de causis.*" *Al-Andalus* 10 (1945): 345-82.

ALONSO, Manuel. "El *Liber de causis.*" *Al-Andalus* 9 (1944): 43-69.

ALONSO, Manuel. "Traducciones del arabe al latin por Juan Hispano (Ibn Dawud)." *Al-Andalus* 17 (1952): 129-31.

ANAWATI, George, C. *Etudes de philosophie musulmane.* Etudes musulmane, 15. Paris: Vrin, 1974.

ANAWATI, Marie-Marcel (G.C.), O.P. *Liber de causis. Traduction française inédite faite sur le texte arabe édité par Otto Bardenhewer . . .* Pro manuscripto. Montreal: Institut d'études médiévales, Université de Montréal, 1950.

ANAWATI, G.C. "Le néoplatonisme dans la pensée musulmane: état actuel des recherches." In *Etudes de philosophie musulmane,* pp. 168-77. Paris: Vrin, 1974.

ANAWATI, G.C., O.P. "Prolégomènes à une nouvelle édition du *De causis* arabe. *(Kitab al-hayr al-mahd)."* In *Mélanges Louis Massignon,* Vol. 1, pp. 73-110. Damascus: Institut Français de Damas, 1956.

ARMSTRONG, A.H. *The Architecture of the Intelligible Universe in the Philosophy of Plotinus: An Analytical and Historical Study.* Cambridge: Cambridge University Press, 1940.

BADAWI, 'Abdurrahmān. *Neoplatonici apud Arabes.* Islamica, 19. *"Procli: Liber (Pseudo-Aristotelis) de expositione bonitatis purae (Liber de causis)."* Cairo, 1955, pp. 1-33.

BADAWI, 'Abdurrahmān. *La transmission de la philosophie au monde arabe.* Paris: Vrin, 1968.

BARDENHEWER, Otto. *Die pseudo-aristotelische Schrift Ueber das reine Gute bekannt unter dem Namen Liber de causis.* Freiburg im Breisgau: Her-der'sche Verlagshandlung, 1882.

BÉDORET, H. "L'auteur et le traducteur du *Liber de causis.*" *Revue néoscolastique de philosophie* 41 (1938): 519-33.

BONCOMPAGNI, B. *Della vita e della opere di Gherardo Cremonese, traduttore del secolo duodecimo, e di Gherardo da Sabbionetta, astronomo del secolo decimoterzo.* Rome, 1851.

d'ALVERNY, Marie-Thérèse. "Anniyya-Anitas." In *Mélanges offerts à Etienne Gilson,* pp. 59-91. Toronto: Pontifical Institute of Mediaeval Studies; Paris: Vrin, 1959.

d'ALVERNY, Marie-Thérèse. "Avendauth?" In *Homenaje a Millas-Villacrosa,* Vol. 1, pp. 19-43. Barcelona, 1954.

DENIFLE, H. and CHATELAIN, A., ed *Chartularium Universitatis Parisiensis.* Vol. 1: 1200-1286. Paris, 1889.

DE VOGEL, C. "Some Reflections on the *Liber de causis.*" *Vivarium* 4 (1966): 67-82.

DORESSE, J. "Les sources du *Liber de causis.*" *Revue de l'histoire des religions* 131 (1946): 234-8.

DUHEM, Pierre. *Le système du monde,* Vol. 4. Paris: Herman, 1916.

ENDRESS, Gerhard. *Proclus Arabus. Zwanzig Abschnitte aus der "Institutio theologica" in arabischer Ubersetzung.* Beiruter Texte and Studien, 10. Beirut: Orient-Institut der Deutschen Morenländischen Gesellschaft; Wiesbaden: Franz Steiner Verlag, 1973.

FRANK, R.M. "The Origin of the Arabic Philosophical Term *Anniyah.*" *Cahiers de Byrsa* 6 (1956): 181-201.

[GILES OF ROME]. *Fundatissimi Aegidii Romani, archiepiscopi Bituricensis, doctorum praecipui, ordinis Eremitarum Sancti Augustini, opus super authorem de causis, Alpharabium. Reverendi fratris Aegidii Bonsi Florentini Eremitae Augustiniani opera nunc imprimendum traditum...* Venice: J. Zoppin, 1550.

GOICHON, A.M. *Lexique de la langue philosophique d'Ibn Sina.* Paris: Desclée de Brouwer, 1938.

GUTTMANN, Jacob. *Die Scholastik der dreizehnten Jahrhunderts in ihren Beziehungen zum Judentum und zur jüdischen Litterature.* Breslau: Marcus, 1902.

HANENBERG, D.B. "Über die neuplatonischen *Schrift von den Ursachen (Liber de causis).*" In *Sitzungbericte der Wissenschaften zu München* 1 (1863): 361-88.

[HENRY OF GHENT]. *Les Quaestiones in Librum de causis attribuées à Henri de Gand.* Critical edition by John P. Zwaenepoel, C.I.C.M. Louvain: Publications universitaires de Louvain: Paris: Béatrice-Nauwelaerts, 1974.

KAUFMANN, D. "Review of O. Bardenhewer, *Die pseudo-aristotelische Schrift Ueber das reine Gute bekannt unter dem Namen Liber de causis.*" *Gottingische gelehrte Anzeigen* 1 (1883): 536-67.

KLIBANSKY, Raymond. *The Continuity of the Platonic Tradition during the Middle Ages: Outlines of a "Corpus Platonicum Medii Aevi."* London: The Warburg Institute, 1939; reprint ed., New York: Kraus Reprint Co., 1981.

KRAUS, P. "Plotin chez les arabes." *Bulletin de l'Institut d'Égypte* 23 (1941): 263-95.

KREMER, K. "Die *Creatio* nach Thomas von Aquin und dem *Liber de causis.* " In *Ekklesia. Festschrift für Bischof Dr. Matthias Wehr,* pp. 321-44. Trierer theologische Studien, 15. Trier: Paulinus-Verlag, 1962.

Ksiega o Przyczynach [The book of causes]. Warsaw: Akademia Theologii Katolickiej, 1970.

LATOR, Steban, "Ibn Sab'in y el *Liber de causis.* "*Al-Andalus* 9 (1944): 415-17.

LEE, Jonathan Scott. "The Doctrine of Reception According to the Capacity of the Recipient in *Ennead* VI.4-5." *Dionysius* 3 (1979): 79-97.

LEE, Patrick. "St. Thomas and Avicenna on the Agent Intellect." *The Thomist* 45 (1981): 41-61.

MUNK, S. *Mélanges de philosophie juive et arabe.* Paris: Vrin, 1953.

MURARI, R. "Il *De causis* e la sua fortuna nel medio evo." *Giornale storico della litteratura italiana* 34 (1899): 98-117.

OSHIKA, K. "Thomas Aquinas and the *Liber de causis.* " *Studies in Medieval Thought* (Tokyo) 9 (1967): 102-22.

PATTIN, Adriaan, O.M.I. " De hiërarchie van het zijnde in het *Liber de causis.* Studie over de vijf eerste proposities." *Tijdschrift voor Filosofie* 23 (1961): 130-57.

PATTIN, Adriaan, O.M.I. "De *Proclus Arabus* in het *Liber de causis.* " *Tijdschrift voor Filosofie* 38 (1976): 468-73.

PATTIN, Adriaan, O.M.I. "Le *Liber de causis.* Édition établie à l'aide de 90 manuscrits avec introduction et notes." *Tijdschrift voor Filosofie* 28 (1966): 90-203. Also published separately: Louvain: Éditions du "Tijdschrift voor Filosofie," n.d. [1966].

PATTIN, Adriaan, O.M.I. "Notes sur le vocabulaire philosophique médiéval." *Revue de l'Université d'Ottawa* 33 (1963): 193*-213*.

PATTIN, Adriaan, O.M.I. "Over de schrijver en de vertaler van het *Liber de causis.* " *Tijdschrift voor Filosofie* 23 (1961): 503-26.

PETERS, F.E. *Aristotle and the Arabs.* New York: New York University Press, 1968.

POULIOT, V.M. and OSHIKA, K. *Liber de causis et Sancti Thomae de Aquino super Librum de causis expositio denuo edidit V.M. Pouliot . . . diligenti cum cooperatione Kazumasa Oshika.* In *Textus philosophici in linguam japonicam translati cura Instituti Sancti Thomae de Aquino de Kyoto.* Kyoto, 1967.

PROCLUS. *The Element of Theology.* A Revised Text, with Translation, Introduction, and Commentary by E.R. Dodds. 2nd ed. Oxford: Oxford University Press, 1963.

[ROGER BACON] *Quaestiones supra Librum de causis.* In *Opera hactenus inedita Rogeri Baconi,* Fasc. 12. Edited by Robert Steele. Oxford: Clarendon Press, 1935.

SAFFREY, Henri-Dominique. "L'état actuel des recherches sur le *Liber de causis* comme source de la métaphysique au moyen âge." In *Miscellanea Mediaevalia,* Vol. 2, pp. 267-81. Berlin: Walter de Gruyter, 1963.

SERRA, Giuseppe. "Alcune osservazioni sulle traduzioni dall'arabo in ebraico e in latino del *De generatione et corruptione* di Aristotele e dello pseudo-aristotelico *Liber de causis.* "In *Scritti in onore di Carlo Diano,* pp. 423-27. Bologna, 1975.

[SIGER OF BRABANT]. *Les Quaestiones super Librum de causis de Siger de Brabant.* Critical edition by Antonio Marlasca. Louvain: Publications universitaires de Louvain; Paris: Béatrice-Nauwelaerts, 1972.

STEINSCHNEIDER, Moritz. *Catalogus librorum hebraeorum in bibliotheca Bodleiana.* Berlin, 1852-60.

STEINSCHNEIDER, Moritz. *Die arabischen Uebersetzungen aus dem Griechischen.* Leipzig, 1897.

STEINSCHNEIDER, Moritz. *Die hebräischen Uebersetzungen des mittelalters.* Berlin, 1893.

SWEENEY, Leo, S.J. "Doctrine of Creation in *Liber de causis.*" In *An Etienne Gilson Tribute,* pp. 274-89. Edited by Charles J. O'Neil. Milwaukee: Marquette University Press, 1959.

SWEENEY, Leo, S.J. *"Esse Primum Creatum* in Albert the Great's *Liber de causis et processu universitatis."* The Thomist 44 (1980): 599-646.

SWEENEY, Leo, S.J. "The Meaning of *Esse* in Albert the Great's Texts on Creation in *Summa de creaturis* and *Scripta super sententias."* Southwestern Journal of Philosophy 10 (1979): 65-95.

SWEENEY, Leo, S.J. "Research Difficulties in the *Liber de causis."* The Modern Schoolman 36 (1959): 109-16.

TAYLOR, Richard C. "The *Liber de causis (Kalam fi mahd al-khair):* A Study of Medieval Neoplatonism." Ph.D. dissertation, University of Toronto, 1981.

TAYLOR, Richard C. "Neoplatonic Texts in Turkey: Two Manuscripts Containing Ibn Tufayl's *Hayy Ibn Yaqzan,* Ibn al-Sid's *Kitatb al-Hada'iq,* Ibn Bajjah's *Ittisal al- 'Aql bi-l-Insan,* the *Liber de causis,* and an Anonymous Neoplatonic Treatise on Motion." *MIDEO* 15 (1982): 251-64.

TAYLOR, Richard C. "A Note on Chapter 1 of the *Liber de causis."* Manuscripta 22 (1978): 169-72.

TAYLOR, Richard C. "St. Thomas and the *Liber de causis* on the Hylomorphic Composition of Separate Substances." *Mediaeval Studies* 41 (1979): 506-13.

[THOMAS AQUINAS]. *S. Thomae Aquinatis in Librum de causis expositio.* Edited by C. Pera. Turin: Marietti, 1955.

[THOMAS AQUINAS]. *Sancti Thomae de Aquino super Librum de causis expositio.* Critical edition by Henri-Dominique Saffrey, O.P. Fribourg: Société philosophique; Louvain: Editions E. Nauwelaerts, 1954.

VAN ESS, Josef. "Jüngere orientalistische Literatur zur neuplatonischen Überlieferung im Bereich des Islam." In *Parusia. Studien zur Philosophie Platons und zur Problemgeschichte des Platonismus. Festgabe für Johannes Hirschberger,* pp. 333-50. Edited by Kurt Flasch. Frankfurt am Main: Minerva, 1965.

VAN STEENBERGHEN, Fernand. *"La bibliothèque du philosophe médiévaliste.* Louvain: Publications universitaires, 1974.

VANSTEENKISTE, C. "Il *Liber de causis* negli scritti di San Tommaso." *Angelicum* 35 (1958): 325-74.

VANSTEENKISTE, C. "Intorno al testo latino del *Liber de causis.*"*Angelicum* 44 (1967): 67-83.

VANSTEENKISTE, C. "Notes sur le Commentaire de Saint Thomas du *Liber de causis.*" *Etudes et Recherches. Cahiers de théologie et de philosophie* 8 (1952) 171-91.

VANSTEENKISTE, C. "Procli *Elementatio theologica* translata a Guilelmo de Moerbeke." *Tijdschrift voor Filosofie* 13 (1951): 263-302; 491-531.

WALZER, R. *Encyclopedie de l'Islam,* Vol 1, 1380-81. Paris, 1960.

WESTERINK, L.G. "Nouveaux liens objectifs entre le pseudo-Denys et Proclus." *Revue des sciences philosophiques et théologiques* 63 (1979): 3-16.

Index of Names

MEDIAEVAL PHILOSOPHICAL TEXTS IN TRANSLATION

Translation #1: "Grosseteste: On Light"
by Clare Riedl-Trans.
This treatise is significant as an introduction to an influential thinker and man of science of the Middle Ages.

Translation #2: "St. Augustine: Against the Academicians"
by Sister Mary Patricia, R.S.M.-Trans.
Augustine aims to prove that man need not be content with mere probability in the realm of knowledge.

Translation #3: "Pico Della Mirandola: Of Being and Unity"
by Victor M. Hamm-Trans.
In this work Pico tried to discover the genuine thought of Plato and Aristotle on being and unity.

Translation #4: "Francis Suarez: On the Various Kinds of Distinction"
by Cyril Vollert, S.J.-Trans.
Suarez propounds his theory on distinctions, a point of capital importance for a grasp of Suarezian metaphysics.

Translation #5: "St. Thomas Aquinas: On Spiritual Creatures"
by Mary C. Fitzpatrick-Trans.
This book falls into two general divisions: an introduction and the translation from the Latin.

Translation #6: "Meditations of Guigo"
by John J. Jolin, S.J.-Trans.
A series of reflections by Guigo, 12th century Prior of the hermitage Charterhouse.

Translation #7: "Giles of Rome: Theorems on Existence and Essence"
by Michael V. Murray, S.J.-Trans.
An essay dealing with the *a priori* deductions of being and its conditions.

Translation #8: "John of St. Thomas: Outlines of Formal Logic"
by Francis C. Wade, S.J.-Trans.
A standard English translation of the Logic of John of St. Thomas.

Translation #9: "Hugh of St. Victor: Soliloquy in the Earnest Money of the Soul"
Kevin Herbert-Trans.
The purpose of the work is to direct the soul toward a true love of self, an attitude which is identical with a love of God.

Translation #10: "St. Thomas Aquinas: On Charity"
by Lottie Kendzierski-Trans.
This treatise is significant as an expression of St. Thomas' discussion on the virtue of charity in itself, its object, subject, order, precepts, and principal act.

Translation #11: "Aristotle: On Interpretation-Commentary by St. Thomas and Cajetan"
Jean T. Oesterle-Trans.
This translation will be of particular value to teachers and students of logic.

Translation #12: "Desiderius Erasmus of Rotterdam: On Copia of Words and Ideas"
by Donald B. King and H. David Rix-Trans.
One of the most popular and influential books of the 16th century is made available here for the first time in English.

Translation #13: "Peter of Spain: Tractatus Syncategorematum and Selected Anonymous Treatises"
by Joseph P. Mullally and Roland Houde-Trans.
The first English translation of these tracts now makes it possible for scholars of logic to better appreciate the continuity of Formal Logic.

Translation #14: "Cajetan: Commentary on St. Thomas Aquinas' On Being and Essence"
by Lottie Kendzierski and Francis C. Wade, S.J.-Trans.
A basic understanding of the relation between Cajetan and St. Thomas.

Translation #15: "Suarez: Disputation VI, On Formal and Universal Unity"
by James F. Ross-Trans.
The study of late mediaeval philosophy and the decline of scholasticism.

Translation #16: "St. Thomas, Sieger de Brabant, St. Bonaventure: On the Eternity of the World"
by Cyril Vollert, S.J., Lottie Kendzierski, Paul Byrne-Trans.
A combined work bringing together the writings of three great scholars on the philosophical problem of the eternity of the world.

Translation #17: "Geoffrey of Vinsauf: Instruction in the Method and Art of Speaking and Versifying"
by Roger P. Parr–Trans.
This text, of one of the most important mediaeval literary theorists, is here for the first time translated into English.

Translation #18: "Liber De Pomo: The Apple, or Aristotle's Death"
by Mary F. Rousseau–Trans.
A significant item in the history of mediaeval thought, never previously translated into English from the Latin.

Translation #19: "St. Thomas Aquinas: On the Unity of the Intellect Against the Averroists"
by Beatrice H. Zedler–Trans.
This is a polemical treatise that St. Thomas wrote to answer a difficult problem confronting his times.

Translation #20: "The Universal Treatise of Nicholas of Autrecourt"
by Leonard L. Kennedy C.S.B., Richard E. Arnold, S.J. and Arthur E. Millward, A.M.
This treatise gives an indication of the deep philosophical skepticism at the University of Paris in the mid-fourteenth century.

Translation #21 "Pseudo-Dionysius Aeropagite: The Divine Names and Mystical Theology"
by John D. Jones–Trans.
Among the most important works in the transition from later Greek to Medieval thought.

Translation #22 "Matthew of Vendôme: Ars Versificatoria (The Art of the Versemaker)"
by Roger P. Parr–Trans.
The Text of this, the earliest of the major treatises of the *Artest Poetical* is here translated in toto with special emphasis given to maintaining the full nature of the complete original text.

Translation #23 "Suarez on Individuation, Metaphysical Disputation V: Individual Unity and its Principle"
by Jorge J.E. Gracia–Trans.
Gracia discusses in masterful detail the main positions on the problem of individuation developed in the Middle Ages and offers his own original view.

Translation #24 Francis Suarez: On the Essence of the Finite Being as Such, on the Existence of That Essence and Their Distinction.
by Norman J. Wells–Trans.
From the Latin "De Essentia Entis Ut Tale Est, Et De Illius Esse, Eorumque Distinctione, by Francisco Suarez, S.J. in the 16th Century.

Translation #25 "The Book of Causes (Liber De Causis)"
by Dennis Brand–Trans.
One of the central documents in the dossier on Neo-Platonism in the Middle Ages. Translated from the 13th Century Latin.

Translation #26 "Giles of Rome: Errores Philosophorum"
by John O. Riedl–Trans.
A previously little-known work that bears new attention due to revived interest in mediaeval studies. Author makes compilation of exact source references of the Errores philosophorum, Aristotelis, Averrois, Avicennae, Algazelis, Alinkdi, Rabbi Moysis, which were contrary to the Christian Faith.

Translation #27 "St. Thomas Aquinas: Questions on the Soul"
by James H. Robb–Trans.
The last major text of St. Thomas on Man as Incarnate spirit. In this last of his major texts on what it means to be a human being, St. Thomas develops a new and unique approach to the question. The introduction discusses and summarizes the key themes of St. Thomas' philosophical anthropology.

James H. Robb, Ph.D. is editor of the Mediaeval Philosophical Texts in Translation.

Copies of this translation and the others in the series are obtainable from:

Marquette University Press
Marquette University
Milwaukee, Wisconsin 53233, U.S.A.

Publishers of:

• Mediaeval Philosophical Texts in Translation	• Père Marquette Theology Lectures	• St. Thomas Aquinas Lectures